A JOURNEY OF HEARING
GOD'S VOICE TO ADOPT

CALLED
to
CASANDRA

HALIE WOOD

Paperback ISBN: 978-1-09836-251-5
eBook ISBN: 978-1-09836-252-2

Printed in the United States of America

Endorsement

" I am SO excited about this book that you hold in your hands....I have known Halie since her college years. She boldly went over to Romania as a single young woman in obedience to God. She has always had such a heart for the orphans, the disenfranchised and the underdog. While over in Romania, she adopted a beautiful young girl, named Casandra. This process was arduous, heart jerking and had many twists and turns. "Called to Casandra" is the story of Halie and her adopted daughter's journey, which is sure to grip you heart, rivet you in your seat and inspire your life. I believe that this book is a must read and will encourage many in the Heart of the Father.

Sean Smith
Author of "Prophetic Evangelism" and "I Am Your Sign"
www.seanandchristasmith.com

CALLED
to
CASANDRA

This book is dedicated to:

Ruth

I will never forget your faithfulness to God and to us.

We love you.

Introduction

"Write! Write! Write!" These are the loud words that filled my mind a few minutes ago as I lay in my bed in the middle of the night in Romania. I stumble to the living room in search of paper and a pen to write, write, write. For some time now, God has been laying it on my heart to tell my story. It's my story with the Gospel woven seamlessly into it. It's a story wrapped in the Father's love.

This story must be told to see how one person's heart focused on Heaven can prove the existence of an amazing, loving Creator. My prayer is that it gives you a boost of courage to follow your God-given dreams. I also pray this courage grows big enough for you to pass it onto the next generation. Courage is a substance that in the midst of fear, can ignite you and move you along into fulfillment that you may not have had otherwise. May you be ignited.

Before I begin my story, I want you to know that a series of compelling, connected events happened in order to create a miraculous result. These circumstances actually happened. God worked in every step along the way, connecting each event, and I was just obedient to His voice. Yes, God has a voice. Yes, you can hear Him if you desire to. I desperately desired to. Now, I'm able to tell you how I was called to Casandra.

Chapter 1

The Provision

When I was 17, an opportunity was presented to me: explore the world and go on my very first mission trip. Ending up in Trinidad and Tobago, a tiny country off the coast of South America, I was there for two full weeks of exploration. My new surroundings were very different from what I was used to growing up in California. Upon landing, we took a drive to the home where we would stay – our place of rest and recuperation from our long hours of ministry. The intense belief in witch doctors and voodoo was evident in all directions. Most of the tropical houses had ripped flags at the end of a bamboo shaft. I learned that these were witch doctor blessings. The more flags you had, the more times you had a witch doctor «bless» your home.

As a Christian, I couldn't help but know that these "blessings" were actually not blessings at all. Tears rolled down my face as the bus took us through the town. There were hundreds and hundreds of these flags on the homes of this island. The people were looking for hope amongst their despair. My heart started to ache for them to know God and find the One true hope. I put all of my effort in those weeks of ministry to show them God's love, and our team saw many give their lives to Jesus.

After that mission trip, I returned home and had to gear up for my senior year of high school. That last year of high school was very profound. God sent me some amazing friends that year who loved God as much as I did. As I approached adulthood, an even greater passion stirred in me to do the Lord's will for my life. The trip to Trinidad and Tobago made me hunger to go on another mission trip. I was hooked! The following year, I signed up to go to New Orleans.

My parents were fine with me going on these trips. They knew me well. As long as I raised the money, their daughter was going to go for it. I had to work hard to pay for every trip. The money from multiple garage sales, candy sales, car washes and support letters usually added up to be enough. During high school I played sports and couldn't find the time to get a job. Every time He provided mission trip money, even right up to the deadline, God made my faith grow stronger.

Just a few weeks after I had graduated high school and before the mission trip to New Orleans, a Christian music festival came to Monterey, California. This three-day festival had dozens of Christian artists come to perform on several stages. My cousin, Willie, had recently given his life to Jesus and called me to see if I wanted to go with him. Willie was a few years older than I was. We were third cousins. My grandma's baby brother was his dad. I have childhood memories with him as always being the funny guy who would make all of the cousins laugh.

Willie was really persistent about me going to this Christian music festival. I wasn't sure I should take the time to go. My New Orleans mission trip money wasn't there yet. Plus, I had already been to the exact same festival the year before. I decided I'd simply tell him I didn't have the money to go. Sure, spending time with my fun cousin would have been great, and I was so glad he found Jesus. The only thing holding me back was spending money I didn't have on festival tickets and a campsite.

Willie was relentless! He called me every day begging me to come with him. On his last attempt, he said he would pay for our campsite, but not my ticket. If I only had to pay for the ticket to get in, then I could make it work. Not wanting to want to let him down, I gave in and told him yes.

Willie lived in southern California. I lived in northern California and the music festival was in central California. He drove up my way to pick me up. As he arrived in my city, his car broke down! I kept thinking that I wasn't meant to go and this was just another sign it wasn't meant to be, but again Willie was still adamant about going. With his amazing problem-solving skills, he asked me if we could drive my car.

Let me tell you about my car. For $600, my dad bought me a beat-up, yellow, 1976 Chevy Nova. With its V6 engine, my car was a complete gas hog, with no air conditioner and a broken passenger side window. We had to beat California's summer heat somehow with no AC. I listed all the reasons why it was unfeasible to take my car, but Willie continued to insist.

Shortly we were off...broken window and all. With only one stop to fill up the tank again, we made it to Monterrey, California. Together we put up our tent and made our way to the festival grounds to see all of the Christian bands playing on the different stages. Honestly, there was still a struggle in my mind justifying spending the money to be there. The struggle slightly lifted when Willie and I started to have a blast!

Looking at the band schedule, we realized that on the last night, both of our favorite bands/singers would be on the same stage. My favorite band at the time was the Supertones, and Willie's favorite artist was Michael W. Smith. Because they were our favs, we had a plan. "Let's get as close as we can to the stage," we decided. As early as we could get there, we took our spots for the day to be up front. We stood behind a wooden board that separated us from the VIP ticket holders. That's as close as we thought we could get.

As we waited in the hot California sun, we were surprised to see a friend of mine from my town who was working security. It was nice to catch up with him. Before our conversation ended and before he got back to work, he told us that he was going to ask his boss if we could sit in the VIP seats. He had noticed many open seats and thought his boss would let us. My cousin and I were thrilled to find out that the boss man gave us the green light! VIP, here we come!

My cousin boosted me over the wooden panel, and then made his way over after. We found open seats and waited for the Supertones to take the stage! We were up and close and had room to dance to my favorite songs. *This is so awesome...*

Before Michael W. Smith came on next, there was a guest speaker: the father of Rachel Scott. Rachel was a girl killed in a school shooting in 1999 in Columbine, Colorado. She loved Jesus very much, and her story touched my life from the day I found out she was shot at her school. She was asked if she still believed in Jesus and shot after her response of, "Yes, you know I still do." I think her story dug deep into my heart because Rachel and I were the same age when she passed away. It had already been over a year since the tragedy had happened.

When her father spoke, I could not help but sob when he told us Rachel's story. I was obviously moved and couldn't hold the tears back. Her story was so inspiring and it was a blessing to hear about her life from her father. After he spoke, I tried to gather myself. That was when a sweet lady sitting next to me said softly, "You are so touched by her story."

"I am. Her story makes me want to do everything I can for Jesus," I said to her as I still continued to wipe the tears from my face.

The sweet lady proceeded to ask me a few questions about what I do and so forth. I basically shared with her that I had just finished high school and would be taking a mission trip to New Orleans soon. I got the chance to ask her questions and found out she had been volunteering at the music festival for many years.

In the midst of our conversation, she said to me, "I feel like I'm supposed to give you money."

Caught by surprise by her words, my mouth must have dropped to the ground. *What? How could this nice lady who just met me want to give me money for my trip?* I gladly accepted her giving heart and gave her my address and phone number when she asked for it. You have to remember that this was back in the year 2000, before everyone had a cell phone in his or her pocket. I thanked her for even the gesture of supporting me financially. Man, was I blown away that God was at work even at a Christian music concert, with a random lady I sat by, in a VIP section I wasn't supposed to be in, that my cousin begged me to go to. Remember, I didn't want to be here because of finances, and here was a stranger blessing me...with finances. Puzzle pieces started snapping together in my walk of faith.

Before Michael W. Smith's set came to a close, I learned this sweet lady's name was Ruth. Ruth kept her word and supported me financially on my mission trip. I started to understand that God was guiding my steps. He was guiding me when I didn't even realize it. I would have never met precious Ruth, if my friend had not been working there. I would not have met her if his boss would have said no to upgrading our seats, and I would not have met her if Willie and I had decided it was too hot to wait for as long as we did. I certainly never would have met Ruth if my awesome cousin hadn't been so persistent. He didn't let anything get in our way, relentlessly adamant we were going to the music festival no matter what. Yes, he was right, and he played a huge part in this story.

That alone makes me see that God is so good at getting His plans accomplished through you and those around you. Ruth obviously had a relationship with God for Him to speak to her like that. Not many people I know would give a lot of money to a young stranger they just met. Ruth is a beautiful gem in my eyes. I had been praying for God to provide for my trips, and He sent the answer by placing Ruth smack dab next to each other. Just like some of you may have heard, if God calls you, He will provide for you.

Chapter 2

The Dots Start Connecting

In New Orleans, I got to see the French Quarter, smell the new scents of the streets and eat a beignet covered in powdered sugar for the first time. We witnessed people longing for answers from tarot card readers and shared the love of Jesus with little kids in the projects. *If they only knew that God could speak directly to them.* Just like my first mission trip, after I came back from New Orleans, I had a burning passion to travel to other parts of the world to share God's message.

The summer of 2000 was when I met another gem in the puzzle. Before the young missionaries went off to the different countries, we would meet in Texas for a few days for team-building exercises, learn some kind of drama to perform on the streets or at a church or discuss the specific way we were going to minister to the country we were going to. This mission ministry had interns who were basically running the show.

Amazing, mission-focused people were there in Texas that summer, and one person I got to know was a guy named Dave. Dave was living in Texas to help the organization as an intern. Dave had a kind heart and a ton of southern hospitality. He was the true meaning of a brother in Christ, always ready to help the missionaries coming through. Dave was my age and was from Tennessee. We were able to hang out some and shared our contact information. I'll tell you a little more about how Dave fits into my story later on. This was the timeline of when we first met.

That mission trip to New Orleans eventually led me to Thailand in December for 10 days. God put a huge passion to go there when I heard of the opportunity. I didn't know how it would be possible though, because the trip was soon and I didn't have the finances. After hearing about it, I laid down in an open field that night, staring at the stars over me, and told God that if He wanted me to go, please provide again. I closed my eyes and imagined the opportunity to travel to Thailand.

The next day, I had a missed call from Ruth. She was calling to tell me that God put it on her heart to send me money again. With joy, I returned her call and shared that just the night before I'd prayed that God would provide for me to go to Thailand. As humble and precious as anyone could be, I could hear the smile in her heart when she responded with gratitude. She had already placed the check in the mail.

I was going to Thailand!

Our team leader didn't hear from our contacts in Thailand for a few days and considered cancelling the trip from the lack of communication. Thankfully, before she made the final decision, she got an email. Southern Thailand had just been hit with a storm and there was major flooding. They still wanted us to come and help, and said that by the time we got there the waters would be receded. They needed our help more than ever.

Our team of ten traveled the great distance to East Asia. As our van blundered through the town on the rough roads, we could see the destruction the flood had caused. Trash piled up in the streets. Water had covered the houses eight feet high, leaving dirty water stains everywhere, inside and out.

During the day, we cleaned houses and stores ruined by the flood, and in the evenings, we went to the university. My friend, Kamerin, and I became friends with a group of university girls who didn't believe in God. They were the sweetest. We shared our stories with them every night for ten days. Kamerin mentioned to them that my birthday was on December 17th (because we would still be there during our trip). The following evening, they surprised me with a Thai birthday cake. When our trip was ending, one of my new Thai friends came to me and said, "I thank God you came here." She then placed a jasmine flower in my hands. That beautiful, fragrant flower was like gold to my heart.

The Thai people we came in contact with were the most generous! We cleaned an elderly woman's house because she was too old to clean herself. We scrubbed the walls, trying to get the water stains off all the way down to the floors. This woman's daughter showed her kindness by purchasing dinner for our whole team of ten. We were taught well; to eat everything before us and as dinner was served, we braced ourselves. Thai food is typically extremely spicy. The two guys on our team decided to step up for us girls – they would eat as much as they could so that we could maintain our politeness! Noticing a ton of food still left, I jokingly told my friend, Clayton, "You're going to have to eat more for us."

"But my mouth is dancing, my mouth is dancing," he squealed in his chair after some water. *This trip is great...*

Kamerin and I had a break before we left, so one afternoon we went frolicking in the jungle close to the place we were staying. As we ran, we pushed tall green plants aside that were in our way. Then, suddenly, we came upon a large elephant. The trunk of the elephant almost hit my nose! Terrified, we screamed, turned and started to run in the other direction. It was hilarious, but scary at the same time. We laughed hysterically after we "escaped," and without words looked at each other with a knowing look: this life with Jesus was the best!

You could say that I started to get a mission addiction. The love of adventure started running through my veins. I loved telling people about God's love and the stories I was making while doing it were amazing. Living a life of adventure was contagious and exhilarating. I also loved meeting other people who were relentless in obeying God like Kamerin and Dave, and meeting people all over the world. *I mean, who gets to celebrate their birthday with a group of girls from Thailand?!*

As soon as that trip ended, I remember waiting to see where else God would send me. All of these places were amazing. They were adventurous; they were real. After each trip, I thought *that was a good trip – God did some amazing things*, but I never felt like it would be a place He would send me long term.

God knows everything about me. Therefore, the question, "What was I made for?" started to shift my prayers. I would say to Him, "God, you know me and You know the whole world. If there is a perfect place You could send me, where I would be used by You to the fullest, please show me!"

Chapter 3

Receive a Heart for Orphans

In my heart, there was always a desire to go to a Spanish-speaking country. For some reason, I thought the next mission trip I should take would be to one, and El Salvador seemed like the place of adventure. I didn't really pray about it this time. It just felt like I had a love for the Latin American countries and their people. It was all set! Or, at least I thought...

A couple of months before the trip date, I got a phone call from the missions organization. The intern girl on the other end of the phone was told the trip had to be cancelled because of political issues in El Salvador. It wasn't safe to go there at the time. Honestly, I was a bit rattled. I wanted to go so badly! Little did I realize my whole life was about to reshape because of that cancelled trip.

After the phone call, disappointment struck. I was not going to El Salvador. Sulking on my bed, I picked up the missions organization's booklet to see where else I could venture. I looked at each country's picture and read about each one intently. The pages slowly turned as I studied at each place closely. Soon, Romania popped up. In the little blurb about the country, it said something about going to orphanages. Boy, did I love kids, and the thought of holding babies who didn't have parents sounded very nice. The urge in my heart revealed the need to go see these babies. I called the organization back and told them, "I choose Romania."

To the airport I went, leaving on another jet plane to another part of the world. I still wished that the jet plane was heading to Central America though. Once again, another trip was financially supported mostly by sweet Ruth. Her faithfulness to God's voice was admirable and I had complete gratitude for it.

The first part of my trip to Romania was harder than expected. Still being a little upset about not going to El Salvador, I struggled with why God had sent me to Romania instead. Yes, the disappointed thoughts came before the trip, but they were heavier when I arrived. It's like my heart wasn't in the right place. Romania was offish to me and so was my heart. Even though I knew I had babies to hold, I kept thinking *I don't really want to be here.*

There was a large group of Jesus-loving teenagers and young adults on this trip. There were 100 of us, and we were split into four groups. The team I was in got the chance to visit an orphanage the day after our arrival. I was certain this was going to be the highlight of my visit to Romania. Being the first of the four groups to visit an orphanage made me happy. Even though

I didn't seem to like the country I was in, I wanted to get going with what God had put on my heart to do: love orphans.

My team entered the building and waited in a room; waiting for our team leader to check us in. Cute little sailboats and décor lined the walls. *Hmm, this isn't as bad as I expected.* Check-in was done, and it was time to enter the rooms where we would find rows of cribs with little eyes peering out from in between the metal rails.

Everyone rushed to hold these precious little ones. I was taking it all in. I'm not sure if it was the fear of my heart breaking more, but there was hesitation in my steps. I slowly walked up to a crib and reached my arms down to pick up a little body. There was a little piece of paper taped to the top of the crib. It read, "Alin."

Alin was about eight months old, and he didn't seem to mind when two new arms surrounded his little body to pick him up. I sat down and continued to cradle him like a caretaker would. That's when I noticed that his body was stiff and awkward. It wasn't how any other baby I had held felt. He wasn't squishy and cuddly. I looked at his beautiful face and tried to make him smile, but had no success. Tears started rolling down my face. I couldn't help it. It was uncontrollable. I tried to stop crying. *How unfair it is for you to see me cry.* I was supposed to brighten his day and bring a smile to his face, yet mine was full of sorrow.

With my entire strength, I held back the tears and held him. But, inside I was breaking.

Oh, Alin, if you only understood what God did in me that day. It was your life that I held when God gave me a heart for orphans.

That evening, we went back to the place where we were staying. I remember talking to my roomie about how much visiting the orphanage impacted me. A heavy sense of love for the orphans hurt my heart. I saw the rows; I saw the cribs. I saw the helplessness in the eyes of the innocent. Most of all, I saw that I could be the answer to one. Shaken by the situation, my heart started to hurt for them, and it was painful. Their cries echoed in my heart and mind, though my room was silent. I decided to make a difference in the situation. With all of my 19-year-old heart, I knew that I would adopt a child one day.

I rationalized my desire with believing one day I would adopt after getting married. My husband and I would decide together when our family would form. It would work together like all of the parts of a clock. I knew in my knower that my future husband and I would adopt, rescuing one child from being orphaned in this world.

Our team leaders informed us that we were chosen to travel to another town three hours away the next day. We had to get up extra early to travel by bus then get on a train to get to the town of Oradea. We settled into bed and I wondered where the adventure was on this trip. My heart was so sad after holding Alin and cold at the same time because of lingering thoughts of Central America.

It was a brisk morning, and the sun was not up yet when we hopped on our bus headed to the train station. My sleepy eyes were trying to stay awake, still not quite over jet lag. When the bus stopped, my team members stood up to file out. As I stepped down from the last bus step onto the ground, I gazed upward, my eyes locking onto a horrible sight. A policeman across the way struck a street child in the face with his open hand. The man started yelling at the child in what was then an unfamiliar language to me. The child held his face and yelled back in agony as he walked in the opposite direction. *What am I seeing?* I could not believe my eyes! Because my teammates behind me were still filing out, trying to get off the bus, there was no time to assess or mentally process the situation. Even if I was able to, what could I have done? The police officer was in uniform and I was just an American bystander who didn't speak the language. We had to catch our train and I had no time to process what had just happened to this child. Our team leader found our train, we grabbed our luggage and piled in to head to Oradea, Romania.

Sitting in a seat on the old rugged train, I stared outside. The sky was gray, and raindrops started to fall, trickling down the outside of the windows. The train smelled awful. Because of the rain, we couldn't open the windows to get some fresh air. There was no getting used to that smell. I felt squashed between two people from my team and we had three hours to go. Each person's luggage was piled up in the middle of the caboose with no room to place our feet comfortably. Then, to add to the misery, a team member came back from the bathroom and told us it was covered in feces. It was going to be a long train ride.

The horrid image of what I had just seen replayed over and over. The scene of the child getting smacked played in my mind repeatedly. It started to get the best of me. Trying my best to shake it off, I squinted my eyes. That didn't work.

Ugh! God, why did You send me here? Why did I just see that poor child get hit? Those questions overtook my mind. After all, I did love children, and to see one get abused was heartbreaking. My mind was flooded with these honest questions and comments to the Lord about what I had just witnessed. My heart began to grow colder and colder. Seeing a child hurt and not understanding why or being able to do anything about it is a horrible, gut-wrenching feeling. The tint on my sheltered, rose-colored glasses was lifting, exposing me to the realities of this dark world and my mind didn't like it.

After drowning in my thoughts, drowning in the images of what I'd just seen and drowning in the nasty smell of this darn train, there was no way I wanted to be in Romania any longer. It wasn't that I was just upset from the injustice of it all, the problem was I had already made up my mind about Romania. Bad things happen in Romania and I didn't like it. *I shouldn't be here.* Seeing the babies lined up in cribs, and then seeing this child getting smacked around was too much for me. During my travels, my eyes had seen some sad situations, but not like this.

I was sinking in this disgust for about two hours. What I saw was bad, but as I was sinking, it started to get too ugly for me to handle. Looking around at my teammates sitting across the trolley cart hoping that someone was relating, I tried to make eye contact with someone who might be feeling my pain. I couldn't tell if any of them were, so my eyes shut and I thought *this is going to be the longest month of my life.* The war was raging inside of me.

After a moment in time, before hitting the bottom of my emotional barrel, I could tell God was trying to get my attention. There was some type of switch that went off in my heart. My mind started to reverse and the Holy Spirit started to work in me. Feeling convicted of my attitude, I realized that the enemy wanted to fill me with anger towards this beautiful country, but God wanted me to love what He loves. He started to remind me of who He is. God also wanted me to acknowledge what He was doing in me. As He started to speak to me my heart, it got lighter and lighter. I felt like Jonah who got swallowed by a whale! Thankfully, I didn't have to get swallowed up by a fish to obey God though. His promise of the Holy Spirit (who was my comfort and counselor) started to lighten my heart. I gladly accepted His gentle comfort.

A little tug on my heart was all that was needed to start feeling a sense of longing; a longing to love what God loves. I can't explain this, other than it was a supernatural experience. Because my heart instantly changed as I listened to Him, my heart could no longer stay in that ugly pit. I wanted what God wanted, but life is not all perfume and butterflies (or elephants and jasmine flowers). Sometimes it is raw, stinky and dirty.

Fed up with the inner torment, I cried out to God. Wanting to love what He loves, I whispered, "Lord, give me Your heart for Romania!"

When we arrived in Oradea, it stopped raining. Rays of the sun tried to peek through the thick clouds. We were picked up by a group of smiley young people. They greeted us and were happy to see us. I was happy to get off of that awful, smelly train! They helped load our luggage onto a bus and took us to our villa where we would be staying. It felt lighter being here and their smiles were contagious.

The heaviness that had been on my shoulders was lifted. I still had the memories, but they didn't taunt me anymore. I was able to move forward in my soul because God's power over the darkness is real. Now, I had the strength to stay on the trip, but before the train ride I was ready to call it quits. He was setting me up for something.

In Oradea we didn't get to visit an orphanage with babies, but we were able to visit one where older children lived. We couldn't communicate with these kids unless we had a translator, but I already knew that love has no language. We spent a lot of time in the parks playing with children and sharing our testimonies of how God changed our lives. My teammates were pretty amazing. I took to a younger guy on our team who seemed to need a little more support. His name was Adam. When we met, I asked him if he had an older sister. He told me no, so I told him he and I were now brother and sister. I quickly learned how to say 'brother' in Romanian (which is 'frate') and started to call him that.

The Romanians who hung out with us were the coolest. Most of them spoke fluent English and it was amazing to get to know them. A group of us got close with a young man named Gelu. He was excellent at translating and started to become a great friend to us. Gelu gave his life to God a few weeks after we arrived, during another team's visit. God was doing amazing things in Romania!

In a park one evening, my team leader asked me to give my testimony. I wasn't nervous, even though it was the first time I had given it. We had a little portable speaker with a microphone and I had a translator.

"Hello! My name is Halie. When I was a little girl my family always went to church. Then we stopped when I was about ten. It was around that time that a friend of mine "taught" me how to steal. We were leaving a store with my dad and she encouraged me to take a confetti popper that was by the exit and I did. We giggled because I got away with it. No one saw! Then most times when I would go to the store, I would get the urge to take something without paying for it. It was a rush! I would steal makeup and hair scrunchies mostly. It felt good right after because I would always get away with it. Then every night my heart would feel so guilty from sinning, usually right before I went to bed. That usually didn't stop me from doing it again though. Every night I had a heavy heart. It wasn't until one day when I was sick of stealing. The momentary pleasure of the rush would die off and I was left with nothing but guilt.

In my room, all by myself, I cried out to Jesus and gave Him my life. I told Him that I didn't want to steal anymore, so I wasn't going to. I cried from the guilt, but I remember knowing I was serious about what I was saying. The next day, I was with my friend and we went to a grocery store. She encouraged me to steal again. I grabbed a Cover Girl cover stick, medium brown, and walked around the store so I could sneak it into my pocket. That's when I heard Jesus talk to me for the first time.

He gently said, "What did you tell me last night?"

All of a sudden, I was convicted of the sin, but I still couldn't let the cover stick go. I remember telling God I wasn't going to ever steal again, but it was hard not to.

Then I whispered, "I rebuke you, Satan, in the name of Jesus!"

My hand dropped the cover stick. It was so intense. My hand let go from the power of Jesus living in me! After that experience I knew Jesus was real and that I wanted to listen to Him. He gave me strength over sin. Because of this experience, I wanted everyone to experience God's power in their lives. God can give you power over sin too if you ask Him into your life!"

As the last words came out of my mouth, I looked into the eyes of those who were listening to me. They seemed to be relating to me. I could see that God was revealing His power to them.

We had serious times and we had comical times in Romania. Getting to know the amazing Romanians was the best! From the orphanages, to meeting new friends and sharing the Gospel, this country had the biggest impact on me so far. I sensed something different for this place than for the other countries I visited, but I took it with a grain of salt while I was there. My heart went from stone cold to a big marshmallow after spending time in Oradea.

Chapter 4

The "Yes" to Go

When I returned to the States at the end of July, all I could do was dream about Romania. There wasn't a day that went by that my mind didn't wander off thinking about beautiful Romanian people, places and experiences. I was sensing that I had to go back almost immediately upon my arrival home. Not wanting to face it though, I pushed the thoughts aside when they came. There was a strong feeling in my heart that the Lord wanted me to return. I couldn't shake it, but I didn't want to face it.

Leaving Romania felt different than leaving the other countries I'd spent time in. After leaving, it was like a piece of me had stayed there. I missed those little orphan faces. I wanted to be with them, and I wanted to share my life with the people of Romania. It's crazy that even though it was the cry of my heart to be where God wanted me to be, I was starting to get a little nervous. *He actually might be answering my prayers.*

About this time, college started. I stayed close to home and went to a junior college nearby. While reading a banner at the school, I found out a new Christian club had started on the campus and immediately started attending it to make some new friends. Their meetings were very impressive because they, too, were talking about having a destiny and seizing the moments God gives us. These young adult Christians were also hearing God's voice like I was. We really dug into how the Bible says we hear the voice of God and how we are called to do great exploits for His Kingdom.

Spending time together at small conferences with mentors who just wanted to pour into us was a blessing. They encouraged us to go after God with their same passion. It was so refreshing to hear someone talk about the things of God that I was starting to experience. It's almost like God had set me right there at the right time to sharpen my spiritual senses.

The feeling that God wanted me to go back to Romania remained strong, but the strongest sense of fear also started to grip me. It was now October, and I was running from His voice. I was being called, but there were so many things I had to let go of. Going on a few trips for weeks at time was all right with me. The thought of leaving for months to a foreign country was starting to get a bit nerve racking. Leaving my family, my dreams and my independence at the door was harder than I thought. This is what I had been asking of the Lord, and when the answers finally started to come, I had a hard time with the reality of it all.

Many doubts and unclear thoughts clouded my mind. I was only 19 years old. *What would I do there? Where was I going to live? How much money would I need? Could I learn another language?* I had to tell my family (who I dearly loved) about my plan, raise the financial support to go and get past the fear striking my mind. I had to obey what I knew God was asking of me. It was a must and it was becoming harder and harder to ignore.

God's will started pulling on my heart more intensely. After ignoring the small pulls for so long, He decided to cover me with His urgency. The urgency happened one particular night as I was talking on the phone with my little brother, Adam (Frate), from the trip. We were reminiscing about Romania, and he then asked, "When are you going back?"

As soon as those words were spoken, it was as if God was asking me through him.

Pausing for a moment, I responded, "Uh, I don't know."

The Holy Spirit tugged and tugged. Knowing I was being summoned by God, I quickly ended my conversation. I went into the bathroom to wash my face before getting to bed for the night. As I rinsed the suds off my face, tears started to come. Looking up at my face in the mirror with my tears colliding with the water, my own eyes revealed that I was running from God. After drying off my face and barely making it to my bedroom, I knew it was time to finally answer Him.

The presence of God was so strong, all I could do was lay on my floor and cry. I cried because it was like God's holy voice was speaking to me. He was speaking His plans for me. Barely being able to contain myself in that moment, an amazing, timely song came on the radio. The radio in my bedroom was usually always on the Christian radio station. It was the perfect song at the perfect time. I knew in the deepest part of my heart that He was asking me to go back to Romania. I got to my knees.

I whispered to Him, "I will go."

Once I said those three words, a strong wave of peace washed over me. All of the wrestling in my mind was gone. It was as if the rope at one end in a game of tug of war was released. God won, but only to place the medal around *my* neck. I wrote in my journal on October 3rd, 2001: "I will be moving to Romania."

Sometimes, when we are wrestling with God about something, and our will finally lines up with His, a peace from Heaven comes in our heart. That's when I believe courage starts to grow in a person's spirit. Surrender is the first step; surrendering to the amazing plans that He has set for you before the foundation of the Earth. It's the moment where your faith is confirmed, and the instant when you have a clear direction to focus on. The fear didn't completely disappear, but God granted the courage to take steps into this plan once I said *yes!*

The next day, I called a family meeting. I can only imagine what each of them thought since we literally had never had a family meeting before. My parents divorced when I was 14 years old. They both lived in different towns. My younger sister, Hannah, was living with my dad and my older brother, Dale, was living with my mom. The meeting place was my mom's living room. When everyone made his or her way to the meeting spot, I made my announcement. I told my family that God wanted me to move to Romania.

The moment was still. I glanced at the tears rolling down Hannah's face. Everyone had a mixed reaction. My brother got upset. It hit my mom just like it hit my sister. My dad broke the silence and simply asked if I was certain. He shared many concerns. This was the year there had been one of the worst terrorist attacks on America. September 11th, 2001, was the day two planes hit the twin towers (plus the Pentagon and an open field in Pennsylvania) and killed thousands of lives. He was my dad, and of course he was worried. By this time, America was in a full-blown war with Iraq. My dad had valid points; he saw his daughter moving closer to the battlegrounds.

To ease his heart, I told him that I was sure. I wouldn't let what was going on in the world dictate God's will for me. At the end of our conversation, I shared with them that I was going to leave in January, I would be gone for six months and I absolutely was certain again that God wanted me to go.

The "meeting" was short, and we talked it through. There was nothing anyone could say to change my mind. Not that they tried to change my mind, but they each had their own way with dealing with the news. Telling them was the toughest part. I felt relieved by just sharing God's plan for my life with them, and it solidified even more that I was going to do it. It's also why I wanted to tell them right away. I didn't want to back out. I told them to put some action to it.

In my eagerness, when there was a break in between a couple of my college classes, I went to the library to look up books or any information about Romania. I grabbed a few books and sat at a table by myself, anxious to learn more about this nation. I remember flipping through one of the books, and something caught my attention. It would be something that would stick out to anyone if it were theirs...I saw my birthday! On that page, I came to find out that exactly eight years after I was born, the Romanian revolution started. Romania was a communist country until this revolution in December of 1989. If you know the history, a Romanian priest started what is called 'the revolution.' This revolution and the overthrow of communism made it possible for me to go to Romania at all. I could tell them about Jesus and not get thrown into jail (like many brave believers did in Romania before the fall of communism).

As I learned more, circumstances like this gave me confirmation that I was supposed to venture off to this country again. God was making it clearer than ever. Confirmations are good when you're about to tread new waters, but more than a confirmation, I felt this was a part of my destiny. The connection with my birthday allowed me to know that I was born for this.

Some sleepless nights came while thinking about the orphans in Romania. Though I didn't know them, God knew them. It's like He was letting me know that I was made to love them. It was obvious by how often they were on my mind. I just knew I was made to hold orphan babies in Romania again.

Eventually, I mentioned to my new Christian club friends that I was going to Romania. They were excited for me. There was a girl who attended that particular day who shared her mission experiences with me. She, too, started to travel the world to tell others about Jesus. Her name was Crystal. It's like she and I instantly had a connection. As she shared, I could see her excitement and love for the places she had visited. I enjoyed every second of her stories and her beautiful heart.

At our next meeting a week later, Crystal came up to me with all seriousness on her face. She looked me straight in the eye and told me that she feels like God wanted her to go to Romania as well. She had never been to Romania before, but God was speaking to her! I agreed that she should come for a visit while I am there. We had just met, but she wasn't a stranger to me. We instantly became best friends. Crystal and I started to hang out every chance we could get. We talked so much that I think we caught up on the 19 years of our lives when we didn't know each other. We even took a two-month kickboxing class together to make sure we spend time together.

Since there were only a few months to prepare, I had to get several things in order, including my travel visa. Being somewhat familiar with visas, I searched the web to see if I had to have one for a six-month visit. At the time, if someone stayed in Romania for six months, they needed one. If I sent my passport off to the Romanian Embassy in Washington D.C., I could get it. As soon as I could, my passport was sent off!

Other preparations were things like purchasing my plane ticket and buying warm winter clothes. Because Romania typically had snowy winters, my California winter attire was not up to par. A nice, big winter coat and some boots were a must!

The time was approaching for me to leave, and my passport had not come back from the embassy. It could have been nerve racking, but I just knew it would come in time. There were a few people who said it wasn't God's will for me to go if I didn't get my passport in time. I would reassure them that it *was* God's will and that it would come! I had so much faith in the truth that I was going to Romania.

The day before I was leaving approached and I still hadn't got my passport back in the mail There was no boarding an international plane without one! I searched the mailbox a dozen times. Remembering that I needed a few more items from the store for the trip, I ran to the store to purchase them in hopes to be able to shove them into my already overflowing luggage.

When I got home from the store, I was in my bedroom with the challenge of cramming my new items into my suitcase. My mom came in with a little piece of paper in her hand. She said the mail had finally come, and the paper was from the post office with my name on it. My eyes read it as quick as can be, and I realized it must be my passport that the mailman tried to drop off. The envelope was certified mail, and my mom didn't hear the knock on the door. We jumped in the car and drove fast to pick up the letter. It was already after 4:00, and we had to get to the post office before 4:30 when they closed. Before the car was in complete park, I jumped out, ran into the post office and handed the note to the post lady behind the counter. She went into the back and handed me a slightly-thick envelope. My heart pounded as I opened it. Reaching in, I pulled out my passport! The passport included a visa to Romania, in line with my destiny.

Chapter 5

Back to Romania

On the way to the airport with my dad and sister, there was a thick, gloomy feeling. There was something different to this drop off because I wasn't going away for a few weeks this time. We parked and they helped me gather my weighty luggage to the check in area. It was also odd because it was the first time I had to say bye to a family member or friend so far from my terminal. The events of September 11th changed the rules, allowing only passengers with tickets at the terminals. Prior to that, loved ones could go straight to the terminal to see you off like my other mission trips were. I had to say goodbye at the security checkpoint this time and walk to my terminal alone.

After checking in, it was time to say goodbye. I hugged my dad, and then reached for my sister. Tears filled our eyes as I squeezed her around her neck, and then I couldn't manage letting her go. It was painful. *How can I leave my baby sister? Will she be okay without me?* I prayed for God to help my thoughts and emotions. I was able to get this far, but as my arms surrounded her, it became difficult to let her go. Out of necessity, I prayed for the Holy Spirit to move my feet, since honestly, I could not move them. Then, suddenly my arms lifted and they were able to let her go. My feet started to move in the direction of the security point, but I didn't feel like I was moving them. Turning around, I whispered, "I love you," and went though.

My gate seemed a mile away in the large San Francisco airport. Once I found it, I sat down in a chair. *This is it! I can do it! I'm going to do it! God, I finally have peace that I will give up anything for You.* For some reason, my heart needed to know that. It was sad to be away from my family, but I had peace that God had an adventure waiting for me in Romania. I jotted my thoughts and prayers to God down in my journal while I waited to board my flight.

In the Bible in Mark 10:17-31, there is a story about a rich, young man who asked Jesus what he had to do to have eternal life. Jesus answered him by telling him to obey the commandments. He told Jesus that he did obey the commandments, but wanted to know if there was anything else. For this rich man, there was something else. Jesus told him to go, give everything to the poor and come follow Him. The Bible says that the man left, sad. His wealth had more say in his life than Jesus did. My say was not wealth; giving my everything was leaving my family; it was leaving my sister into God's trust. When I was able to go through the security checkpoint, I had a rush of joy throughout my body. The joy wasn't because I was leaving her, it was because that was what I had still been holding on to. Trusting that God would take care of my family was a release on my heart. *Obedience is bliss!* Some people do drugs for some kind of rush, but I follow Jesus! It's hard to explain if you haven't experienced it. There is such freedom in obedience. Though I was crying, I was not sad. Though I had tears, I had such an unexplainable sense of joy.

You see, whether you are a Christian or you don't know the Lord, there is a simple reality that lies within the human. It's called a 'soul.' That soul is crying out to become alive with God's Spirit. The Spirit only comes by knowing Jesus. Because Jesus died and rose again, the very essence of God can live inside of us. I want to speak to that part inside your heart, crying out to know your Maker. I speak to the part of our being that cries out to be loved unconditionally. We have a good God with good plans for us. In order to enter into our destined adventure, it's wonderful to follow Jesus with nothing holding us back.

I went to Romania that cold winter in January 2002. I was 20 years old, with about $2000 dollars to my name. I'm certain that Ruth had given me half of that. The only thing I knew for sure was that the Lord had granted me a heart for orphans. My plan was simple: go to Romania and love orphans. The Lord had started speaking to me during the couple of years prior to this, so I was assured that it was His voice. My passion became to love the least of these.

The long flight was fine. After I gathered my luggage on a cart, making my way to the exit, I saw a man holding a piece of paper with my name on it. A friend who I met on my first trip orchestrated a ride to take me to Oradea. Her dad was a pastor of a local church. He even helped me find a place to live, and I trusted that they had it sorted out for me. When I stepped out of the airport in Budapest, Hungary, a cold breeze wrapped around me. Now onto a three-hour drive to Oradea.

There was a thin layer of snow covering the ground. It was going to be fun living in a place where it snowed for the first time. I stared out into Hungary's frozen tundra, hoping to get to Romania quickly. My driver wasted no time, and eventually we were at the border. After reading about communism, the border crossing always made me nervous. The armed police with their wool hats made for a scene out of a scary movie. I handed my driver my passport, so he could hand it to the police officer. They opened the truck of the car and looked over my luggage, all while speaking Romanian. I'm not going to lie; it's a bit frightening. It was such a relief when I had my passport back and we drove away.

Within a few minutes I could see we were in Romania. I could see the tall apartment buildings and breathed in the familiar smell of it. The picture of this beautiful place was stuck in my mind since I had left it. We drove through the town, and eventually pulled up to the place where I was to lay my head for the next six months. The driver helped me drag my suitcases to the second floor. With a loud bang, he knocked on a door.

The door slowly opened. From behind it was a blonde-haired, blue-eyed young lady named Natasha. She was a few years older than I was. She was very sweet and helped me in. I walked into the little, beaten-down apartment. I was tired from traveling, but took note of my new, limited home. The tile in the entrance was half missing. The walls of the two-bedroom apartment were all a stale pink, with the exception of the bathroom.

In the bathroom, the tiles were also coming off the floor and surrounding the tub. In the kitchen, sat an undersized, white fridge and a small table with two chairs. There was a small balcony off the kitchen that contained the kitchen stove and sink. My bedroom had a dresser and a couch.

Natasha had graciously cooked a meal for the two of us that evening. She cooked rice, with ham and an egg. I sat across from her as we ate in our pink kitchen. I didn't eat red meat normally, but I smiled and ate what was on my plate. Natasha knew very little English at the time, and I obviously didn't know Romanian besides the couple of words I learned the previous summer. Our conversations were quite amusing. It was interesting how we communicated with each other, but we did!

Before bedtime, Natasha showed me how the couch in my bedroom folded down into a bed. These sofas were typical in Romania. She gave me a thick winter blanket and sheets for the night. I made my bed and put on my warm winter pajamas.

As I lay there in the dark silence on my new couch bed, I was a bit afraid. A small tear rolled on the side of my face down to the pillow. My whispers to a loving God brought peace to my heart until I was able to fall asleep. I knew I would be okay; I just didn't know what the next day had in store.

Chapter 6

One Door Closes and Another Opens

The bright sun pierced through my bedroom window the next morning. It was SO bright. I jumped out of bed and peered out my little window to see my new surroundings in the daylight. The snow was obviously still there. My eyes took a while to adjust, since the light reflecting off the snow made for a brighter light than I was used to. It was beautiful! The joy that came to my soul that morning was fresh and uplifting. I was so happy to be back!

In my eagerness to get to work with whatever God had planned for me to do, I wanted to meet with the pastor to see if he could help. Thankfully, the church was close to the apartment. Natasha and I got ready and headed out. We walked on a dirt road in slushy snow just about half of a mile to the church. The pastor met us with a smile in his office and asked me what I wanted to be doing during my stay in Romania. I assured him that I wanted to work in the orphanage with orphans. He was nice and immediately found the number in a notebook in his desk to call the orphanage.

He spoke with someone over the phone in Romanian. He nodded a few times and I understood the word "da" which means yes. I was a bit antsy waiting to hear the details. After he hung up, he kindly told me that they were not allowing any volunteers into the orphanage to help.

There was an imaginary rock that hit my gut. *Wait a minute! How am I supposed to love orphans if I can't go to the orphanage?* I was quite perplexed that their answer was no. God wants me to love orphans. How was that supposed to happen if they wouldn't let me in the orphanage? It didn't make sense, since I felt very strong that was what I was to do while I was there. The door was shut. I had to remind myself, many times, that I did trust God.

The pastor had an idea to call the children's hospital because he knew there were babies there. He picked up the phone again and called the children's hospital. After he hung up, he shared that they agreed to have me. He told me they would be expecting me the next day and to go to the seventh floor.

So, it wasn't working exactly how I had planned it, but all I could do at the moment was assume I was to help at the hospital. Even though it wasn't where I thought I would be going, I was here because God had sent me. The best thing I could do was remind myself of this.

Clearly, I didn't know how to get around the town yet, so Natasha became my tour guide. The hospital was way on the other side of town from my apartment. Instead of taking a taxi, she showed me how to take the little tram that goes through town. The tram reminded me of an above ground subway. When we were on our last stop to get off, she pointed to a tall concrete building. She revealed to me that this was the children's hospital. It looked like a giant, ten-story grey Lego that was out of place. It faintly looked like a prison, with a gate and a guard at the entrance watching people as they came and went.

Honestly, walking through those gates and into the hospital was one of the most culturally-shocking moments I have ever had. Passing the guard and making our way into the front door, the first thing I noticed was how dark it was. There was not one single light turned on inside the building. The rays of the cold winter sun were the only lights, dimly peering through the windows.

We were headed to the seventh floor and decided to take the elevator. We saw one across from the stairs, and it was the tiniest elevator I had even seen! We started to press buttons in this tiny space, but it wouldn't move. A nurse noticed we were trying to use it, so she used her authorization key to allow it to work. She asked where we were going and Natasha answered her. We giggled on our way up to the seventh floor because we didn't know only authorized employees were allowed to use the elevator.

To our joy, when we got there, we met the doctor who spoke perfect English. Natasha was happy to have shown me the way and left. Doctor Prada was a smart, steady and vibrant woman. She showed me around to the section we were in. It happened to be the intensive care unit for babies. She gave me a white cloth outfit to wear when I was there, and then started to show me where the children were. I couldn't help but notice the same paint-chipped cribs that were at the orphanage I visited on the trip before. The little sheets were also tattered and torn on most edges. I smiled when I saw tiny bodies wrapped in them.

Dr. Prada explained to me that these babies had parents, but their parents had to work and couldn't be with them. It was hard to wrap my brain around that fact. I also knew I wanted to be with babies who had no parents, but thought it might help these babies to have me there with them while the hospital staff was busy. Like I said, I trusted God.

Sometimes when things don't work out the way we think they will, we just need to trust Him. The Bible says in Psalms 37:23 that the steps of a good man are ordered by the Lord. Each step I took to the children's hospital, I thanked Him for ordering each step. The sacrifice Jesus made for me made me righteous and whole. I believed that God did ordain my steps even when they didn't make sense.

I diligently worked with children and babies in that run-down children's hospital. It was fun getting to know some of the nurses and letting them practice their English with me. I didn't venture too far from the seventh floor – the section I was delegated to. *After all, these Romanians were fresh out of communism,* was a thought that always floated across my mind. I didn't want to overstep any boundaries. There was no doubt that God wanted me there, but that didn't stop me from wondering why He had given me a heart for abandoned and neglected children.

Each day I pressed in for an answer. The desire in my heart grew to hold a baby who had been orphaned. Even so, I kept my focus on the open door I had at the hospital and tried to make the best of it. Eventually, I became acquainted with how things run in their culture. I began to understand how behind times Romania's facilities were. As I mentioned, the hospital rooms were dark and dingy. The metal cribs the children were in were very old with white paint chipping off each and every one of them. The sheets and blankets were tattered as if they had been there for ages. The rooms were painted odd colors for a hospital (most were painted a faint turquoise). Even the medical equipment seemed to have been bought centuries ago. The building was built strong, but everything in it was not keeping up with the time.

Glass bottles were filled with the babies' daily meals of milk and soup. When it was feeding time, the nurses would prop the bottles up with the crib and a cloth. I sort of get that they didn't have time to hand feed them, but when I first saw this, it was like a law had been broken as far as I was concerned. *This is not how it's supposed to be.* Even though I was only 20, I knew tiny babies should be held when they are eating. Maybe it's a justice heart that runs through me and it's not a huge deal to others. Either way, every time I saw a bottle propped up and a baby turning its head forcibly to finish their bottle, I would pick them up to offer comfort. Then they needed to be burped too, so their tummies didn't get upset. I would pick them up, hand feeding them one at a time, if possible.

In my free time, I would learn the language, read my Bible and Christian books and hang out with my new Romanian friends. I also spent a lot of time praying for my friends, family and Romania. I became acquainted with some of my apartment neighbors and was still full of the lingering excitement of following God's plan for my life.

My apartment had no washing machine or dryer. I had to learn how to do laundry like many did in this beautiful country. I would fill the bathtub with water, pour in some laundry soap and then add my dirty clothes. My arms were used as the machine to get them as clean as I could while I listened to tapes to help me learn Romanian. The hardest part was when I had to ring them out to dry. That took some practice and muscle. And, imagine how long it took for them to dry in the cold winter!

Every once in a while, a street child would roam the apartment complex begging for food. Then a horse and trailer would come by with a gypsy family. In the back of the carriage would be little dirty children eating whole cucumbers. I was experiencing another culture, another world.

During this time, the early 2000's, you could not find very much food prepackaged in Romania. If you wanted to eat, you had to cook things from scratch. You couldn't find things like Rice a Roni or cans of soup. It was clean eating. Our trip to the outside market to buy the fresh food was a neat experience in itself. There were tables full of fresh vegetables and fruit all around. Each table you walked by, the sellers asked if they could help you. It wasn't too hard to convert pounds into kilograms, and the tapes I was listening to sure helped me learn to say different fruits and vegetables in Romanian. Needless to say, I started to learn how to cook real food the real way. I would watch Natasha cook many nights and that helped!

One unforgettable night was when Natasha was teaching me how to cook a Romanian dish – stuffed cabbage. The language barrier still plagued us at times, and she was trying to tell me that the water needed to boil. As she spoke in Romanian, she motioned with her fingers, making a boil movement. I realized what she was doing and said, "Oh, BOIL!" We laughed that evening so much! Language didn't get in our way. She learned a new word in English and I learned one in Romanian that I would never forget: to boil. That night, we decided to be each other's teachers. We would sit together and learn each other's language and laugh!

When I came to Natasha's apartment, she had only two items in the fridge. She was able to make a meal from practically nothing. I started to buy all of the groceries. Thirty dollars a week bought a surprising amount of food. When I first met my new roommate, she was quite thin. After a few months of me living there, Natasha started to look like a healthy young lady. By paying her $100 rent, she was able to buy things and do things she wasn't able to before. During this time, the average Romanian family was living off of a mere $100 a month.

I enjoyed going to church and hanging out with the teenagers in the youth group. Even though I was older, there were others that were older too, and we kept hanging out. One evening, a girl named Lavinia, Lavi for short (who I had seen a few times), came up to me. I had no idea that she could speak English and she spoke it so fluently. She told me that her birthday was coming up and that she wanted me to come to her party. I eagerly accepted her invitation.

From that day on, Lavi and I became the greatest of friends. For hours we would sit on my couch bed and talk to catch up on our whole lives prior to knowing each other. Lavi was so bright and taught me Romanian history and how the real story of

Dracula came out of Transylvania, Romania. I never cared much for history until I had her as my teacher. She showed me her school and took me to the youth group at her private school's church. Romania was being good to me.

Chapter 7

Best Friends in the Making

The weather started to change and the snow started to melt. The trees along the city streets started to blossom, but my heart was still weary. My passion to be with the unwanted babies wasn't changing. My time was coming to an end here, and I needed answers. With heavy shoulders, I took a walk right outside the edge of town, feeling frustrated. I felt like the Lord told me to look up at the city. I saw the homes and the buildings; it was a whole city that needed the love of God. My heart started to break for this place even more. I wanted them to understand God's love and freedom. Inside I wrestled with the idea that maybe God was giving me a heart to the *spiritual* orphans. Maybe for those who didn't know him as Daddy? I didn't know.

A huge highlight during this time was Crystal actually coming for a visit. She had her own set of hurdles to get there, but she came. Her stay was only a week, but we totally had a blast together for those short seven days. I loved showing her around and taking her to the children's hospital. She got to wash clothes by hand and all! She got the chance to see all the ins and outs of my life as a missionary to Romania, that's for sure! She brought me some of my favorite food items, like peanut butter and items to make rice crispy treats. It was fun watching our Romanian friends eat a marshmallow for the first time in their lives. She also brought a pack of water balloons, and with the kids in our apartment building we had a water balloon fight with giggles that lasted all day.

Crystal's boyfriend, Josh, insisted that she bring rain ponchos with her the day before she left. She tried to assure him they wouldn't be necessary, but packed them anyway to make him feel helpful. Out and about one day we continued to joke about how we should bring the ponchos just in case it did rain. We laughed, but Crystal threw them into her backpack anyway so she could at least tell him we tried to use them.

It was a sunny day with no sign of rain or clouds, so we didn't think we would have use for them. I took her to a little village outside of Oradea to walk around. I wanted to make sure she saw some sights before she left, especially the beautiful lotus flowers that grew in that area. We took a bus to and from the village. On our way home, the sky quickly started to change. Ominous, dark clouds were rolling in. We got off the bus and saw the rain clouds taking over the sky. Crystal opened her backpack as quickly as she could and grabbed the rain ponchos. We put them on, and instantly it started to pour. It was one of the funniest circumstances I had ever been in! Our sandals were soaked, but the rest of us was dry. Somehow Josh really knew we would need them.

That night, we called Josh to tell him about our adventure that day, and we made sure to tell him the story of our sunny day becoming a rain storm, and how his ponchos kept us from getting soaked!

One of my favorite things to do while living there was to make sandwiches, go around passing them out to the street kids and tell them that Jesus loves them. I took Lavi with me my first time doing this and wanted to share the experience with Crystal. She has such a huge heart for children. That day we went to a little gated area that had a few poor families living there. We passed out the sandwiches and played with the kids. Sometimes that is all it takes!

Like I mentioned, this girl was my best friend. We enjoyed every moment with each other for that week and my heart was sad for her to leave. I wasn't sure when our next adventure would be, but I hoped it would be soon.

Chapter 8

Skip Back to America

My six-month, God-ordained stay was coming to an end. I had a talk with my new amazing friend, Lavi, about coming to America for a visit and she agreed. My heart was to share more of my life with her. We had to apply at the American Embassy in Bucharest and get approval for her visit. They granted her the visa, and we booked the flights together. It was her first time flying and her first time to do many things.

I'll never forget my return home. I was so amazed at how straight and clean America's streets were! My dad and sister were at the airport waiting to pick us up. I left them in January and now it was July, and I was thrilled they were there for my arrival. It's funny – my sister said I was 'stinky' when I came home. I guess when you wash your clothes by hand for six months, they don't smell that great...

Lavi had never seen the Pacific Ocean or any ocean before, and watching her as she saw it for the first time was a real treat.

She ran straight for that ocean when we took her to see it! I had my camera in hand and wanted to capture this pure moment of joy. Lavi ran straight in, clothes and all, wearing the biggest smile anyone ever saw! Her time was mostly spent hanging out with new friends, seeing the sights and eating peanut butter and jelly sandwiches. In Romania, a jar of peanut butter was nowhere to be found, and this girl fell in love with it.

It wasn't until Lavi flew back to Romania that I started to feel home sick...for Romania. It was weird. Since I wasn't holding orphans while I was there, I wanted to be home in California. Now that I was back, I wanted Romania again. *What is going on?* I loved the days I spent as a missionary in Romania, but my heart ached to not do what I felt called to do.

Soon, I started another semester of college. It seemed as though I didn't quite fit in anymore with the American ways and mindsets. After my first trip to Romania, things that used to matter a lot didn't matter as much anymore. My eyes opened to America's excessive consumerism. The difference between what we think is important vs. being exposed to the great need in this world was daunting. I just witnessed families living off of a hundred bucks a month, and we can drop a hundred bucks in a hot minute on something ridiculous.

Being in college and working again in America was fatiguing. But, I did it. I was blessed to find a job as a nanny for two twin boys, and I signed up for a full load of classes that semester. I did my best to look forward and focus on my studies.

One day, while sitting in my child development class toward the middle of the lecture hall, my friend from my old youth group sat next to me, wanting to catch up on my time away. We muted our voices when our teacher began talking. "Hello, class. Today I have a film that I'd like to show you." The lights dimmed and the film began…and there they were. The white, paint-chipped cribs, tattered blankets, rows and rows of precious children without families. Before the film's narrator announced it, I knew these were Romanian orphans. Tears came rolling down my face as I watched. My heart was breaking again! I could feel the emotional pangs of pain going throughout my body, especially in my chest.

In that whole lecture hall, I was the only one crying. There were still babies over in Romania lined in cribs that I NEEDED to love on. I needed to be Jesus' arms to hold them tight, to sing to them, to pray for them, to believe in them! I can't explain the overwhelming conviction of compassion that flooded my whole body. My compassion still needed action.

My friend leaned over to me and nodded his head up and down, seeing how God was touching my heart.

But, wait a minute! I was just there! I was obedient, trying to do what my heart and God were telling me. It just didn't make sense. *Why was I not allowed in the orphanage in Oradea?* Honestly, I'd had several conversations with Jesus about *why…I do not understand this whole dilemma* many times. *Why did it hurt so bad to not be able to hold them?!*

Like my situations before, I started to ask Him more often, "God, why didn't I get to hold an orphan? I went to Romania to hold the babies who didn't have anyone to hold them. Why does my heart still yearn to hold one? I don't think that I heard you wrong, but I don't understand. Do you want me to go back?"

Six months is a long time to live in an unfamiliar country. Six months was a long time to have a desire in my heart, hoping that each day it would be fulfilled. Six months is a long time for it *not* to happen. I mean, I was in a country with thousands and thousands of orphans. Believing that I was made to hold one was undeniable. My reaction to the orphanage video made me desire to love on the orphans even more! The video made me realize my time in Romania was not over. My heartstrings were pulled once again.

It didn't take long for me to figure out that I was supposed to go back, again! This time, I felt like I would be there for three months. This time, I really asked God, "What in the world do you want me to do there this time?" Loud and clear I heard Him say, "I'll show you when you get there." It was like He was saying He had a surprise for me. My ears were tuning into His voice. Whatever it was, I was ready for it!

Also during my prayer time before I left, I sensed I was going to visit Germany. This thought was strange, but it kept coming up when I would pray. Germany became a place I knew I would visit, but there was only one problem. I didn't know one single person who lived there. For a month or so I pondered the thought and knew if God was putting Germany on my heart for a reason, then He would allow me to go there. Never before had I desired to visit Germany until then.

The night before I left for Romania this time, my dear friend, Dave, called me from Tennessee. He just randomly called to check up on me and asked how I had been. I told him everything…about Romania, that I was going back to Romania the next day and how I thought God may want me to go to Germany. I laughed when I told him about Germany though, since I had no connection whatsoever with anyone in Germany. "Halie, you're not going to believe this, but…" He went on about a married couple, youth pastors in Germany, who had just stayed the night at his house *the night before*! I found out that they were missionaries from America who worked with youth in Germany. *God, You are so amazing!* I was so excited, and he promised to send me their information through email. God was definitely up to something! The random call from Dave, the youth pastor in Germany who stayed with Dave the night before…thank God he called before I left!

I arrived in Budapest the following January. This time it felt like I was home. Without dispute I was being torn between my nation and this one. I came out of the terminal, grabbed my luggage and headed to find my ride. This time my ride was not here to greet me. I couldn't find my driver holding a piece of paper with my name on it. I double-checked with Lavi before I left, as she made the reservations for a driver and had all of my flight details. I decided to wait for a while. My ride was most likely just running late. After a while, it started to get very late and I started to get scared. *God, please give me a ride to my town.* I paced the small Budapest airport looking for my ride for over an hour.

While I was pacing the airport once more, I saw a man who looked familiar to me. *Where have I seen him?* As I looked at him, he looked Romanian, and I tried to figure out how I may know him. It took a minute, but I remember seeing him at a youth group Lavi had taken me to. It was the youth pastor of the private school that she went to! With nothing to lose, I got enough guts to speak to him.

"Sir? Are you from Oradea?" I said shyly.

"Yes!" He replied.

"I remember hearing you preach at a youth group my friend brought me to. I cannot find the ride that she sent for me. Is there any chance you have an extra seat for me to Oradea?"

"I am waiting for a team to arrive from America. We have a 12-seat van and we are expecting 11. The extra seat must be for you! Here they are now!"

I looked over and saw a group coming through the terminal with luggage. Not only did this team go to Oradea, but they also stayed only about a quarter mile from my apartment. God provided once again, and my assurance that God was looking after me was growing.

My miracle ride soon arrived in my town late that night. I stared at the familiar, tall apartment buildings that covered the city. The snow covered the city like a fresh blanket, giving the city a clean, crisp look, typical for a Romanian January. As I looked out the van's window, I saw the cable tram riding by with the last few passengers. Oh, how many times I had taken that cable train back and forth to the children's hospital. I remember thinking *to be in God's will is the greatest feeling ever.* The adventure, walking by faith, and this destiny was my future. I was home.

Chapter 9

My Little Surprise

Natasha had moved but my new roommate was a lady named Olga. She agreed that I could move in with her. Olga was tall, with brown eyes and hair, and had a brilliant mind. She spoke four languages fluently and was a Christian as well. I slept soundly that night being back in my old Romanian apartment. After waking up, I couldn't wait to get back to the children's hospital. It was the only thing that I knew to do. I knew I was hearing Him clearly and trusted that He would direct my steps if I just got moving. I grabbed a banana for breakfast and walked to the tram to get to the hospital.

Reaching the hospital, I hurried to the seventh floor where I had worked before. I remember thinking *I don't know what else to do except for doing what I did before.* Going to the orphanage was still a wish, but I knew God said He had something special for me.

My legs hustled up to the seventh floor. A little out of breath, when I reached the top, Doctor Prada was right there. She greeted me with a big smile and handshake. She was very happy about my return. Since this unit was the intensive care unit, she was in a hurry, but said:

"Halie! You're back."

"Yes, can I still help?"

"Yes, and I have a baby for you. I would like you to take care of her. She was abandoned in another town, but they brought her here because she is very sick. We had to resuscitate her just yesterday. Come with me!"

Okay...pause! What!? An orphan!? "I was just here for six months and didn't get to hold an orphan! But, there's one here now, and you are taking me to her? Did you just say that her heart just stopped beating yesterday?! And you saved her life?"

My face filled with a grin. As you can imagine, I could go on and on about the explosion of thoughts that flooded my mind right then. As I followed that busy doctor to the child's room, I knew this was a very special assignment. I was about to meet a baby who God wanted me to love. Pure joy covered my entire body.

Dr. Prada opened the door, and there she was! A little baby with no mommy, with no daddy, with no place to call her own. My heart felt like it was about to jump out of my chest.

This little baby's sweet head turned slowly towards the door when we walked in. Her eyes were big and brown, with no smile on that precious face. Her sickly little body was hooked up to what seemed to be ten IV's. She just stared at me and our eyes were locked. As soon as my eyes meet hers, I felt my heart beat one humongous beat. I swiftly walked to her bedside. Doctor Prada unhooked her IV's so I could hold her. She could see my intensity; I could hardly wait to pick this child up. *Oh, my heart!* I was about to hold what my heart has desired for so long. The doctor handed her to me, and little did I know what was to come!

It was like when a mother carries their beloved child in their womb for 40 weeks. The anticipation. The joy. I struggled for a year, wondering if I'd heard the Lord correctly, telling me to love the orphan. Here she was. It may have taken a year, but here she was. My little surprise. My arms were finally satisfied.

Now that I think about it, it's like when new parents see their newborn baby for the first time. All that they've been through…the preparation, the labor, the sweat, the duration of the pain. Then the pinnacle moment comes: the baby is placed into the arms of their mother. This is exactly what it felt like. I had anticipated this moment for so long.

As I cradled her little body in my arms and remember telling her, "You are so special! God sent me all the way from America to hold you until you get better and until He sends you a family. It's going to be okay. I'm here. God has a special plan for your life." Her big, brown eyes stared at me, she didn't smile and she didn't make a noise. She just stared at me.

Oh, the Lord is so good! His Word will never come back void. Waiting for her to be placed in my arms was worth the heartache; a whole years-worth of heartache I had felt not being able to hold an orphan. I looked at her crib and found a tiny paper with writing that said: "Casandra - October 3rd, 2002." What a beautiful name someone had given her. *Casandra...*

I held Casandra with the greatest joy I had ever experienced. I thought how wonderful it was for God to send me to love her. Knowing she was my mission, I would do everything in my power to take care of her. At that moment, she was my purpose.

God had spared her life! He knew He'd be sending a crazy, young girl from across the world to nurture Casandra. I immediately sensed that God's hand was on this baby's life. It had to be. One of two circumstances either happened. Either God's hand is on her life and she just got sick. God knew they would bring Casandra to Oradea where I was, and that's why He said to come back and spared her life. Or, maybe a way more intense option: the enemy saw the greatness and the likeness of the image of God in her and tried to take her out. He may have had the notion that a girl across the world was on her way to pray for her and protect her. By sheer fear, he sent the sickness to take her life, but God had people there to bring her back.

After my visit with her, I went straight to the store to buy bottles and formula. I was somewhat familiar with the process of feeding time in the hospital, but I know newborns were hungry often. I wanted to make sure she was fed properly. My plan was to do everything in my power to keep her safe and nurture her back to health.

Every morning, I would heat up the water in my apartment, add the formula and head to the hospital. As I mentioned, the hospital was on the other side of town from where

I lived. It took the city's tram, then walked about a half of a mile (usually in the snow). By the time I got to the hospital each morning, the bottles were the perfect temperature. I knew that the hospital was feeding her, but I thought one or two extra bottles a day might also help.

Though she was never crying when I got to her, when I gave her the bottle, she was always extremely hungry. If you have ever seen a hungry baby only a few months old, not allowed to eat every two to three hours (like they are supposed to), it can be a bit heart-wrenching. Casandra would drink the bottle fast – in only a minute or two. Her little lips moved as fast as they could to get the nutrients down.

A couple of days after I met her, her vitals were improving and the hospital staff moved her to another unit. There was another baby in her new room, and they even shared the same crib. Interestingly, her crib mate's name was Alin, just like the first orphan I held on my first trip to Romania. Because it was winter, the room was always cold. The two of them were always wrapped tightly in a few thin blankets. These two precious babies would just lie there alone if I wasn't there to keep them company. Sometimes I held both of them at once. They were both so light and frail that it was easy to do so.

When I had just Casandra in my arms, she would never smile. She just stared at my face. I always had the impression that she was thinking, "Who are you? Who are you to me?" The question would come up, but never allowed my mind or heart to follow that train of thought very far. I would never let it wander past my immediate focus: to spend time taking care of her.

My many attempts to put a smile on her face didn't work. I would goo-goo and gaga in baby talk and make silly little noises. Nope. She would just stare at me with those big eyes. As matter of fact, she hardly cried or made much of any noise. It was the beginning of my "institutionalized baby" voyage and understanding what they are like. Their crying mechanism starts to shut down. Sadly, they learn early that crying doesn't get anyone's attention. I made up my mind that I would pray for her every day, multiple times a day. I began to pray for two specific things over her: joy and strength. These seemed to be the two virtues that she needed the most.

Parents understand that taking care of a newborn is tough work. They get fussy, hungry and need to be changed. They get tummy aches, can't sleep well sometimes and need to take in their environments in order to learn and develop. My heart broke to know that most of the babies who I saw in Romania's institutions didn't get their immediate needs met. Sure, they were getting fed on a rotation, but if they never had two loving arms holding and comforting them, that's simply injustice to me.

Chapter 10

God Opens and Closes Doors

Another day dawned and to the children's hospital I went, as usual, to hold Casandra. When I walked into her room, my eyes fixed onto her crib, but she wasn't there. I looked around the rest of the room to find her and she wasn't there at all. Worry started to fill my mind and spike my blood pressure. *Where is she?* I tried to find Dr. Prada for help, but was unsuccessful. The nurse down the hall didn't know where she was either. Frantically, I started to look through each door on the floor, searching for those big brown eyes. After looking through every room, I still couldn't find her.

On this particular day, I couldn't find anyone who spoke English to help me. As a matter of fact, there were only a few personnel at the hospital that day. Help was scarce. I decided to just search for her. With each step, I prayed that God would help me find her. I went down a floor to search through each room, and no Casandra. Then, I went down another floor and another. My heart started to race. My determined steps turned into a jog, and then a run. After checking every room on the seventh, sixth, fifth and fourth floors, I ended up on the third floor, still searching. I entered one room that was pitch black. My eyes couldn't see a single thing. I made my way to where I knew a window would be and pulled open the curtain. I turned around and as my eyes adjusted, I could see a crib with two tiny bodies.

Casandra and Alin were fast asleep in that dark room. They were both wrapped in tight blankets in the same crib. At my first glance it looked like Casandra wasn't breathing. I picked her up as quickly as I could, and she was limp. Her head rolled backwards and her eyes wouldn't open. Tears rolled down my face and I shouted, "Casandra! Casandra!"

She was passed out, and I honestly didn't know if she was alive. I checked her pulse and found one. Then, I noticed that she had some kind of thick oil on her head. It was if someone had drugged them to sleep. After several minutes, Casandra finally opened her eyes a tiny bit, but only to close them again. She couldn't even manage to open her eyes for a second. Anger and sadness rose up within me. What was worse is that I had no idea how long they were actually left like this. I was so thankful I found her and glad I hadn't given up my search!

I held precious Casandra, and I kept wiping the tears as they rolled down my face. My eyes were locked on her little chest to make sure she was breathing. She was so tired and still so frail. The light coming in from the pulled back curtain didn't seem to bother her. I just had to be sure I could see her breathing. Alin moved his tiny lips to yawn, and I could see that he was fine. I picked him up with my open arm.

There I was, now on the third floor holding these two. Questions and thoughts of injustice filled my mind. *Why is this happening to them? Why was the room so dark?* A baby should never be left for hours in the dark during the day without any human contact. It felt so inhumane, and that's why it hurt so much.

I cried as I held them, deeply thankful they were found. They were still sound asleep for as long as I was there. As long as I knew their little bodies could feel the warmth of another human being's arms, I would hold them for as long as I could.

My prayers became more earnest after experiencing this day. I was continually asking God to give Casandra and Alin loving families. This day did something to me. When I couldn't find her, it was awful. When I found her and she was in the state she was in, it was awful. Alone is the worst place a baby should be. Somehow having little Alin right next to her was a sliver of comfort.

The next day when I came through the hospital, Casandra was alone in her new crib. She was awake on her back, and most importantly, not limp this time. Alin, though, was no longer there. I don't know where he went, but that dreadful day was the last time I saw him.

I lifted Casandra up out of the crib, cradled her in my left arm and fed her a bottle from my backpack. Now there would be two bottles for her since Alin wasn't there.

A lady who worked in the unit sat at a desk outside of this room. When my day was up, I walked past her.

"There are other babies in this hospital. Why do you only go to this one?" she mumbled, with a heavy accent.

"I didn't know where the other babies were, and Casandra is the one Dr. Prada took me to, to take care of." I said caught off guard.

She just shook her head back and forth.

The weight was heavy. The oppression was real. It started to get to me. I was strangely tired all the time. The darkness of the hospital was getting to me. It's like Satan's thumb was pressing on the atmosphere of the children's hospital where so many little ones were. Why was he so afraid of them?

On the other hand, where were the other people who could be holding these babies in their free time? Where were the kind-hearted Romanians in the city of 200,000 people? Did they know that there were little ones who needed help on the other side of that hospital gate? The questions were many, but I didn't have answers.

I am a problem solver at heart, so I started looking into private orphan care places to see if they could take Casandra out of there. At the time, I was very unfamiliar with the laws and procedures for what happens orphans in Romania, but I was determined to find an answer for Casandra's sake.

A few days later, a woman who worked at the children's hospital told me that they were going to move Casandra to the state orphanage. She was talking about the same state orphanage that I was denied access to go to the previous year. I was thankful that she shared this information with me, although it wasn't the best news. I took a deep breath, preparing myself for this next obstacle. In no way was I doubting that God brought me to Casandra. After seeing God orchestrate everything so far, I was ready to see another miracle.

My assignment was to take care of *this* baby. Now they are moving her to the place that a year prior said I could not enter. I had no doubt God would create another miracle. Not only were they moving her, but the next day. I had no time to prepare, only to pray. That night, I thanked God that He was going to send me into that orphanage. This was exactly my perspective in my prayer.

"God, I am Your child. I am Your daughter. You own everything! You can harden hearts and soften hearts. You own that orphanage. You want me to take care of that little baby. She is leaving there in the morning. I know they once said that I may not enter, but I thank you that they *will* allow me to now. I thank you for the favor on my life and the plan that You have with Casandra. I am asking that You would soften their hearts and allow Your daughter to enter Your orphanage. In Jesus' Name!"

This prayer was said out of an inheritance, knowing I was the daughter of the King. I knew He heard me, and I knew He would have to do a miracle.

The next day, I grabbed my sweet Lavi to come with me to translate. I wanted her with me just in case there was no one who spoke English at this state orphanage. She was willing to come, and I remember sharing with her that their answer was going to be a yes! We got there and passed the first guard at the gate. I have no idea what is up with guards at the entrances of these places, but here was one here, too. Lavi spoke directly to him and she was as bold as a lion. He agreed to let us enter.

Once we entered through the gate, I looked up at this massive, yellow, historic building, trying to envision babies on the other side. Not just any babies, but my Casandra. I came into the director's office and, to my advantage, she spoke English. I explained to her how I had been taking care of Casandra at the hospital and how I wanted to continue taking care of her at the orphanage. It did not take much convincing. You could tell she was a woman who wanted to do the right thing. She had a gentle spirit, not at all like I had imagined.

We could tell that she pondered what I was asking. It may have even been deep thought, but we gave her the seconds she needed to find the answer. The answer was a yes! She wanted a copy of a form of identification. I brought my passport with me by chance and she made a copy of it for her records.

After the copy of my passport went through the machine, she immediately took me to see Casandra. I remember walking up a flight of stairs and into a portion of the building. I had such joy in each step to see her because God allowed me to be there. I remember the nurses looking at me, wondering who I was and what was I doing there. They may have also wondered why I had such a cheesy smile on my face!

Though the orphanage was still dark, thankfully it wasn't as dark as the hospital. The windows all had white, embroidered curtains that the light could shine through even if they were drawn. I looked around and immediately noticed that this was a better place for her to be.

The director opened a door and there she was. I was united with Casandra after only one night to see her big brown eyes. I picked her up in my arms and rocked her saying, "God has a plan baby girl. He is looking out for you. I am here to love on you until He provides a family for you."

It was then when she started to smile.

If they had allowed me to be there during my six-month stay, I would have gone straight to the orphanage on this trip instead of to the children's hospital. In doing so, I would have missed that whole month with this precious baby girl! God had it all planned! He wanted Dr. Prada to take me to her. He wanted me to know for sure that she was my plan.

That was just one of the many miracles that the Lord did! I started to notice more and more how He truly was ordaining my steps. I recognized each strategic person He was putting in my path to make His plans come to pass. Prayer and confidence in who you are in Him makes a significant difference. He is the Master Puzzle Maker. He created everything to fit perfectly together. Every step, every no, every yes…every person had meaning. Do you see it!?

The previous year, when I was obedient to come to Romania, Casandra wasn't even born yet. In the Bible, Jeremiah 1:5 says, "BEFORE, I formed you in the womb, I knew you. Before you were born, I set you apart." This part of my story really demonstrates God's knowledge of us before we are born. It also shows how much He loved Casandra. This part of the story clearly proves that He knows our future. It confirms the Father's great love for us, that before we were even born, He loved us. He loves us just as we are before we can even prove our love to Him.

Casandra was a tiny, helpless baby girl. There was nothing she had done to be abandoned by her parents, and nothing she had done to gain this new favor in her life. His eyes were directly on her, and His plans were orchestrated and played out even before I had a clue about what was going to happen.

Not only did I get to go to the orphanage, but I could go whenever I wanted! They did not put any restrictions on when I could come – any day of the week and any time. God did that. All of these amazing things started to happen. One of the most amazing miracles was that my soul was at peace. I was made to love an orphan. I was finally loving an orphan.

God had made a way when there seemed to be no way. I didn't skip a beat in being there for Casandra. Every day that I was in Romania, I went to love on Casandra. I also got the chance to love on every baby in her section. Most of the time the nurses would sit in the lounge drinking coffee and smoking cigarettes. When it was time to feed and change the babies, they would. Their cloth, tattered diapers didn't hold long, and most of the time their bottoms had rashes and sores.

While the nurses relaxed in the lounge, I would pick up Casandra and the two-of-us would pray for each baby. I would place her little hand on each of them and we would pray. Her now huge smile would bring smiles to the babies. Sometimes there were almost 40 babies at a time and sometimes only 15.

They kept the orphanage fairly clean, but that didn't stop roaches from scurrying across the floors every once in a while.

One of the wonders I saw in this orphanage was when an infant would be in their crib, lying on their back, staring up into space. Most of them were like this often. There were no cute decorations or mobiles floating above their head, just plain, white ceilings. Like I mentioned, all of the walls were painted white. Sometimes, if I looked just at the right moment, a baby would start to giggle and move as if something or someone was above them making them laugh.

I remember reading the Bible in Matthew 18:10 where it says, "See that you do not despise one of these little ones. For I tell you that their angels in Heaven always see the face of my Father in Heaven." How awesome! In the deepest places of despair in this world, He is still in charge and has angels entertaining orphans.

Chapter 11

A Nudge to Germany

One evening, I went to an internet café to check my email. Dave had sent me the contact information for the missionaries in Germany like he said he would. "Joe and Shelly, missionaries to Germany, email address ____." I wasn't sure what they would think, but I wrote them anyway. I typed up a quick, friendly note, mentioning how I knew our mutual friend and how I believed God had given me the desire to go to Germany. Their response came the following day, and they welcomed me into their home. They let me know what dates worked best for them, and I bought my bus ticket to Germany when the details were worked out.

I felt much better about Casandra being in the orphanage instead of at the children's hospital. They were feeding her much more here, and at least I knew she was getting some kind of human contact. I even stopped bringing her bottles from home since she didn't need them anymore. She was being fed and changed on a normal rotation. The thought of being away from her for a week was tough, but peace filled my heart. *She is going to be fine.* Soon, I was on a bus for a 24-hour ride to Germany.

Upon my arrival in Frankfurt, not really knowing what to expect, I got out of the bus and looked around for the most American-looking man I could find. During my search, I saw a man looking around for probably the most American-looking young girl he could find. Approaching him, I asked, "Are you Joe?" It was him.

Joe had come with his niece, Cathy, who was my age. We had a pleasant conversation on the way to a nearby town where they lived. In no time I realized this family was amazing! Their love for this nation and for God radiated from them. They shared with me that they were taking a team on a mission trip to the Philippines in April and invited me to come. "Wow, thank you. I would love to, but I have to pray about going."

When I started to pray, I asked God very specifically if He wanted me to go to the Philippines. I wasn't hearing an answer. At this time with my relationship with Him, I really felt that I could just ask and He would tell me. This time though, I wasn't hearing anything. Just silence.

Germany was a neat place. It had a rustic charm like Romania. As we rode along on the cobbled streets, I imagined the men of long ago setting each stone in their perfect place. The streets were clean and everyone was really nice. Staring at the Germans' lips as they spoke their beautiful language was fascinating. *If only I knew what they were saying.* It was fun to be spoiled for a week with great food and being with a God-serving family from America.

Near the end of my visit, we went to Joe and Shelly's church youth group. During the prayer time, I prayed again about going to the Philippines with them. On my knees I heard the Lord speak to me. He said, "Go with Joe." It was His sweet voice and it was VERY clear.

After the youth service, Shelly asked me if I knew whether God wanted me to go to the Philippines with the team or not. I said, full of excitement, "God just spoke with me and said, 'Go with Joe,' so I guess I am going!" Shelly celebrated by giving me a high five!

Later that evening back at their house, Joe received a phone call from another leader who was going on the trip. It seemed to be a very important call. He was in the other room for some time and came out with a sad look on his face. He shared with me that the other team leader, Winston, had received a phone call from the contact person in the Philippines urging us not to come. I cannot recall exactly why, but some kind of political situation was happening and the locals didn't think it was safe for us to come.

Joe and Winston decided they still wanted to go on a mission trip, but it just wouldn't be to that location. Winston was from a country on the tip of South America – Suriname to be exact. He had many contacts there. After some deliberation, they decided the team would go to Suriname instead, since the door had closed to the Philippines.

After Joe told his family and I the news, I spoke up. I shared with them how it all made sense. God didn't tell me to *go to the Philippines*. During my prayer time, I asked God, "Do you want me to go to the Philippines?" I didn't hear an answer until that night, but it wasn't a *yes* or a *no*. He simply told me, "Go with Joe." ☺. Not only was I going to embark on another trip to another corner of the world, but I was also hearing God's voice clearer. I wasn't just sensing it; I was hearing exact words. Looks like I was going to South America.

With their awesomeness, this lovable family took a moment to thank God for His divine direction over the mission trip and my life. Joy (and a little bit of silliness) took over for a few minutes. We could feel God's Spirit guiding us. We sat in their house, praising God, sharing life together. I was beyond blessed to share these moments with them. Their love for God and the world was contagious.

Joe and Shelly had two sweet children – about five and seven years old. They had brown eyes, brown hair and lovable spirits. Shelly shared with me the date they got married and her children's birth years. As I did the math in my head, it all didn't add up to me, and I could tell Shelly was trying to make a point. Her daughter's birth was before she and Joe got married. I looked at her, puzzled. *Why is she telling me this?* Then, she smiled. "Our children are adopted!"

This family listened to me intently as I spoke of Casandra. It was as if they started to love this baby and hearing her story. They were just people who loved Jesus and loved His little ones, too. It was fun to see their family blended together through adoption. It was thrilling to know that a little impression to travel to Germany allowed me to befriend this amazing family.

You might be thinking *who cares that you went to Germany?!* This story is all going to connect, I promise. Bear with me...

My short time in Germany was over and I was excited to get back to Romania. Upon my return, I was delighted to see that Casandra had been well cared for. The nurses were talking to her. She was growing little by little. She still had tiny, thin legs, and her little cheeks that hung over near her lips needed to be filled with baby chub.

I continued to speak life over her and love her as if she was my own. Like I said, Casandra was getting fed every feeding rotation, and instead of the bottle being propped on the crib, it was in my hand holding it to feed her. While she was in my arms, words cannot express the love this child brought to my heart. I started to feel uneasy, knowing my time with her was coming to an end.

Because my next mission stop was South America, I needed to head back to America first to get things in order. I was trying to book a flight to South America from Romania, but things just were not working out and I did not have peace about it. I knew I was meant to go home first, but the thought of many hours on planes flying back and forth was a bummer. I did not want to leave Casandra at all and my emotions were all over the place concerning her.

Desperate to find a home that could adopt Casandra or a foundation willing to take care of her until she had a permanent solution, I started looking into places. I heard of a nice place with a positive reputation; they took good care of orphans in homes. They had two locations in Oradea, and each property had multiple homes. Each home had about ten orphans and a set of parents who took care of them. I was able to call and set up a meeting with one of these couples.

My taxi pulled on the property slowly. *This place is nice, these houses are cute,* I thought to myself. I knocked at the door and the sweet Romanian couple met me there and welcomed me in. The home was pleasant and I inspected the place with both my eyes and my heart. I explained the situation to them and asked if they would be willing to take Casandra until God provided a family. They agreed, but told me they were unable to take her permanently. I was okay with that; I just needed to know someone was watching over her. In the meantime, Lavi had agreed to visit Casandra until they moved her out of the orphanage.

I can't quite remember when my last visit was with Casandra this trip. I think my mind didn't want to remember it anyway. All I know is that I put a lot of love into that little girl who God put across my path. My search for a family to love her as I did was unsuccessful before I had to leave, but I felt like I put things into place. At least that gave me a little peace, even though my heart broke every second I had to be away from her.

Chapter 12

The Yes in Suriname

The next portion of my life was a whirlwind. I flew to California only to be ready for Suriname in a week. I gobbled up as much family time as I could get, although I'm pretty sure they thought I was crazy. I held my baby nephew in my arms and gave him as many hugs that could fit into seven days. I also had a little time with Crystal. The day before I was leaving, she came over with a bag of toys to give to the kids there. One large duffle bag was all I could bring and it was already stuffed. Somehow, I still shoved the little bouncy balls and toys in. Crystal was always thinking of the children and how they are blessed by the simple things in life.

Time to go! One duffle bag packed and ready to fly again… check. My travel itinerary included flying back to Europe (to Amsterdam), and from there flying back across the Atlantic to Suriname with the team from Germany. The reason why I had to go back to Europe was to get a visa for Suriname. The Suriname embassy is in Amsterdam. My flight landed, and Joe had it set up for a girl who volunteered at a YWAM (Youth With A Mission) base to pick me up and take me to the embassy. The sweet YWAMer (as I call them) walked me around the city to the Suriname Embassy for the visa, and then back to the base to stay the night. The rest of the team had taken a train from Germany to Amsterdam's airport, and we met up at the airport the following day.

Eventually, we all arrived in the beautiful, tropical nation of Suriname. The leaders of the trip were still Joe and Winston. I remember the great anticipation about what God was going to do here. Of course, I could never shut up about this little Romanian baby and my love for her. I'm sure I rambled tirelessly, but most of the team listened to me and wanted to hear about her. Not being with Casandra made my heart hurt, so I guess I made up for that by talking about her endlessly.

This trip was unlike the other trips I had taken. Our team consisted of two Americans, Joe and I, a man from England, and the rest were Germans. We had a little multinational team. Suriname was stunningly beautiful. The tropical weather, the people and the adventure we got to experience…all amazing. We took canoes down rivers to be with a tribe, the Saramaccas. We ate with them, fellowshipped with them and shared God's love with them.

One day on a walk, we heard some other village kids shouting, "RACA, RACA!" Our translator told us that they were shouting, "White people! White People!" Yep, that was us. I saw little black eyes peering through some bushes. They wanted to come see us, but they didn't know what to do. *We're not scary.*

Come see me. With my hand and a smile on my face, I urged them to come closer. Shyly and slowly they came one by one, unsure of what would happen. Then, one brave girl reached for my hand and I held it. Not more than a minute later, I had three kids on each arm walking with us through the rain forest.

On another day, we went for a walk to the market and I was taking in all of the newness. The language, the smells and the weather – it was all different. We walked past a house and there was a little girl about three years old sitting on a chair on her porch. *I bet that is what Casandra will look like at that age.* This little girl had olive skin, big brown eyes and dark hair with two curly pigtails. She was adorable. God had His way of reminding me of Casandra around every turn, as if I wasn't already thinking of her constantly. Though I was an ocean away from her, even a little Surinamese child reminded me of the orphan I was made to love.

It could have been on this walk or another one, but Joe and Winston came to me and told me they wanted to talk to me when we got a moment. At first, I was trying to think of something I did wrong! *Why do both of my leaders want to talk to me about something?* When we had a chance, they took me aside from the team. Very seriously, they looked me in my eyes and asked me a question.

"Halie, we have something to ask you. We'll get straight to it. We want to know if that's all the Lord wanted you to do for Casandra? Was it for you to just take care of her for those months?" Joe asked.

Without saying the exact words, I knew in my heart what he was implying.

Joe continued, "When you talk about this baby, Halie, you LIGHT UP."

I motioned my face towards Winton for confirmation, and he looked at me and shook his head up and down to agree with Joe's words. There was also a surge in my being when Joe said, "light up."

That's when it hit me. Did I? Did I light up when I talked about her? Our conversation was short. Joe had a sense that God might be up to more than I believed. He was the first person who outwardly said it, asking if I was supposed to be the one to adopt Casandra. I didn't exactly know how to answer them. "I want to hear from God on that, and I don't feel done taking care of her."

Did God want me to adopt her? I took care of her when I was there and prayed for God to send a family to her. It was the first time that this topic was really spoken out loud. Fleeting thoughts of it had crossed my mind, but I never gave serious thought to the possibility of it *actually* happening.

I had to know if there was more. I had to know! Like I mentioned earlier, I hadn't let my heart go there. Now, it was as if my two leaders were giving me permission to go there. It's like they both understood that if you are doing something that God calls you to do, His light shines through it and through you.

At this point in my walk with Jesus, I knew I was hearing His voice. I knew that if I only positioned myself before Heaven, He would tell me if this was His will and plan. Wow, could it be I was made not only to *love* an orphan, but also to make one my own? To wipe the word 'orphan' far from her? *Could it be possible?*

Our team had free time later that day, and I went by myself into my room where we were staying. I knelt on the mattress on the floor, positioning myself the best I could to hear from Heaven. My prayer and cry went something like this.

"God, do you want *me* to adopt Casandra? Do you want ME to?"

With every fiber in me calling out to Him, I heard His voice.

He asked, "Do you want her?"

I cried, "God, You know that I want her!"

As clear as day and with a stern tone He said, "Then go get her!"

Without a shadow of doubt, I am absolutely positive that Heaven hit my heart when I heard the voice of the Lord say to *go get her*. It was as clear as clear can be. I heard Him. With every circumstance I'd experienced until this point, His voice was like sweet honey to my soul. Nothing could convince me otherwise.

I jumped up off the mattress after my conversation with God, still wiping the tears from my face, and hurried to tell the team. The team was scattered throughout the kitchen and living room for lunch. "I just heard from God. I'm supposed to adopt Casandra!" Joe, Winston and the team were thrilled; thrilled that I was going back to get her. Everyone smiled and celebrated the news. The Lord surrounded me with people who believed this was going to happen, and He knew I would need them at this moment of decision. My leaders didn't bat an eye. It's like they already knew I was going to get her. Remember the great joy I experienced at Joe and Shelly's house? Well, it returned times a million right then.

My mind started to process all of the things I had to do. *There is so much I will have to take care of.* Now I knew why I had to go back to America first. It all made sense why I didn't have peace about staying in Romania and flying directly to South America from there. I'm sure I had some paperwork to gather in America. I already missed Casandra, but after this point, the feeling became different. My heart ached for my child. She was mine...*my child*.

I went back to America with one focus: to get ready to go back to Casandra as soon as possible. I knew there would be documents and other things to gather up to start an adoption process. In the meantime, Lavi still checked in with Casandra. She would call me after a visit to tell me how she was. When I told my mom and dad the news, they both said they knew it; they knew I would eventually realize I was to adopt her. I honestly was surprised for a few reasons. First of all, I was only 21, wasn't married, and that meant going back to Romania when I had no idea how long it would take. But, thank God my family was on board. Just knowing they were okay with it was a tremendous support.

There was a lady from America living in Romania who worked in the social work field. I don't know how our paths crossed, but I emailed her for help. She ended up giving me a list of documents needed to adopt Casandra. Let's call this woman Mabel. Mabel didn't seem to flinch when I told her I was going to adopt Casandra. It was nice to have someone who understood the paperwork and process. After I had the list, I started getting it all done in the short time that I had.

While away from Casandra, I missed her more than anything. The pain in my stomach from being apart was torture. Before I went to bed one night, I prayed that God would give me a dream about her. *God, at least let me dream about her to ease the pain.* To dream about her would be good for my soul. I fell asleep and woke up the next morning to the noise of my dad placing something on my dresser. When he saw that he had woken me up, he apologized. Actually, I was glad he did because I was just dreaming of Casandra. Because of the noise he made sneaking in, I was able to remember my short dream.

In the dream, I was driving a green truck. I pulled up to my dad's house and put the truck in park. I got out of the truck and went to open up the extended cab. Out of the extended cab came Casandra from a booster seat. I helped her out of her seat and the two-of-us started to walk up to the porch holding hands. In the dream, Casandra was about three years old. She was in summer clothes and had the curliest hair ever. As we walked up to my dad's house, the dream ended. It ended because I woke up when my dad placed something on the dresser.

The dream was such joy to my heart! I got out of bed to see what my dad had placed on my dresser for me. It was a pink envelope. I opened it and it was a Mother's Day card to me from him. It was Mother's Day that Sunday morning! How sweet of him to think of that. That gesture from my dad and the dream from God gave me such strength until I held her in my arms again. It was kisses from Heaven like the dream and the card that encouraged me so much, reinforcing that the adoption was going to happen.

Before my return, I was able to spend some time with Ruth. She invited me to her church one evening when they were having a guest speaker come named Heidi Baker. I had heard about Heidi before, but never got the chance to hear her speak in person. Heidi was a missionary in Mozambique, Africa, and had amazing stories of her encounters with God on the mission field and her love of the African people.

Crystal came with me and we filed into a small church in the Bay Area. I don't remember what Heidi spoke about that day. I'm sure it was something amazing about passionately loving God and people. What I do remember, is that when she ended and started to pray, I was compelled to go down to the altar and pray. Her passion from the Holy Spirit drenched the place and I had to do something.

I knelt at the altar thinking about Casandra, of course. I knelt at the altar thinking about the many babies left there. I knelt at the altar and thought of Casandra's birth mom. There was so much resentment in my heart towards her, even though I didn't know anything about her. This is the first time I have mentioned her birth mother. I'm going to be very vulnerable.

Sometimes when I thought of her, anger burned. Like I said, at this point I knew nothing about her other than she was of Roma (Gypsy) descent (because Casandra was). Times when Casandra would need extra care, I would think *how could someone leave this beautiful child? Are you even thinking of her?*

For every time she needed someone, you could have been there. My unhappy thoughts of this deadbeat mom surfaced from time to time. I imagined an old, mean woman, like from a Disney movie. Someone like a wicked stepmother type...only someone like that would abandon his or her child.

Then, all I could do was cry now at this altar. The tears fell and continued to fall as God was changing my heart. Instead of being angry with her birth mom, my heart changed at that altar. Instead, I started to become thankful for this woman who gave me the greatest gift: Casandra. There were no words coming out of my mouth, just the Holy Spirit covering me in repentance. Just like when God changed my negative heart about Romania on the train ride to Oradea, in that little church God changed my heart about Casandra's birth mom.

Chapter 13

Momma's Coming for You

Back to Romania I went, and this time with tons of baby girl's clothes in my suitcase. My emotions were high and the plane couldn't fly quickly enough! The lady sitting next to me must have been surprised when she asked where I was going and what I would be doing there. My story poured out for the next 20 minutes. It just hurt so much to be without Cassandra, but when the smile came on my face from talking about her, the pain eased. I got to the orphanage as soon as I could the following day. There was definitely a skip in my step.

My mind carries such a sweet memory of this day. The director was happy to see me back and showed me to the new room Casandra was in. I followed behind her to my baby girl who I missed more than anything. She was on the same floor, but just got moved to the opposite side because she was now eight months old.

When I walked into her room, Casandra was on her stomach facing the door. When she saw me, the biggest smile erupted on her face and she started to inch her body to the end of her crib in my direction. This mommy picked her up and whispered, "I'm here. Mommy's here to get you." Holding her tight to my chest, I just breathed. There were lots of hugs, kisses and moments of just staring at her in awe; the awe that she was finally in my arms again.

It was like an emotional exhale, and then a new breath finally filled my lungs. It felt like I had taken a deep breath when I had left her, never letting go until I saw her again. That smile on her face was worth a million bucks. She was still there just waiting for me to come back for her. She was waiting for her momma just as much as her momma was waiting to return.

Casandra had not changed much. She was a little bigger and was moving around some. The only thing really different about her was that her hair was gone! She used to have a long, straight clump in the middle of her head. Now her hair looked like someone must have shaved it off.

After my visit, I shared the news with the director and the social worker at the orphanage. They were delighted to hear my plan to adopt her. I immediately started to ask for the list of items that needed to get done to get the ball rolling. My plan was to get this adoption going quickly, but it was very important to get her out of the orphanage and home with me during the process. In my mind, I estimated we would be Romania for approximately a year, so I wanted to press on and get everything accomplished.

About a week after my reunion with Casandra, the social worker came to me with unfortunate news. It was my worst nightmare news. She told me the Romanian government was putting a new ban on people from other countries adopting Romanian orphans. Romania was changing their adoption laws that would directly affect us. If you weren't Romanian, you couldn't adopt from Romania.

Could this really be happening? Am I really hearing this? I just got back to start the process to adopt her. This was the most crushing news my ears could hear. It took a moment to shake off the despair before it took grip. Hope had to be more powerful than what I had just heard. One thing was certain though, God had already revealed His plan to me. There was no convincing me that just because a law changed that she wouldn't be mine. She was already mine and I was 100% sure of it. God was going to have to do a huge miracle, and my heart had the faith to know He would.

My faith had been growing a few years prior. If God could provide a ride for me at the airport when I didn't have one, He was going to provide a way for me to adopt her. If God was going to take me to South America to reveal to me through leaders that I was supposed to be more involved in Casandra's life, He was going to do it. If my passport arrived the day before my plane departed to Romania, He would do it. God had built up my faith through all of these circumstances. Nothing was impossible with my God! He had worked everything out so far, even the smallest of details!

At this point I KNEW I was going to adopt her. I KNEW what God had spoken to me. Nothing could shake that even if nothing was making sense. Here was a whole nation that had decided to say "NO." There were laws being put into place that exact month to close all international adoptions. I knew in my knower that with a mighty God, it would be accomplished anyway.

This report completely contradicted what God had said to me. It would have been easy to just throw my hands up and admit that I hadn't heard God's voice. The only problem with that option was that I *knew* I heard His voice. There was not a speck of doubt despite this opposition. I could have gone back to America and said, "It's not possible," but this girl knew that with God ALL things are possible (Matthew 19:26). It was possible because I knew how big of a God He is. He is the God that defeated death and was resurrected. It was possible, through that resurrection, for me to believe that the mountain in front of me would have to throw itself into the sea to get out of the way of God's plan. By my own strength, there's no way it would happen. But with Him, surely it was possible. I just knew it. It's that plain and simple.

Instead of going back to America on the chance that this whole adoption thing was all some terrible mistake, I dropped to my knees and shouted to God with tears rolling down my face. I wasn't shouting because I was mad at Him. The shout was acknowledging that He is the One I turn to when a twist in my life happens. I admitted that I didn't know what was going on. I admitted that I *did* know His voice. Boldly to His throne

I entered and told Him that it didn't matter what obstacles were set before me. I knew Casandra was my daughter. The tears came, but thankfulness came to Him from my lips in advance that one day she would have my last name. I started to cry out for the miracle only He could do.

I always knew that if a plan was from God, then it would take God for it to happen. I was in a perfect place, a wonderful, terrifying place. I was now commissioned into a place of complete surrender before God, but positioned to fight for victory. It was going to take God to do the miracle, but I still had to step into the miracle every second of the day, knowing any moment it could happen.

To fulfill my wonder, I peeked through my journal one night to skim across what God had been speaking to me. I was tickled to see that Casandra was born a year exactly after God spoke to me to go back to Romania the first time. This sweet reassurance was confidence to my soul. *There will be a way.*

It wasn't just Casandra and I who were affected by this law. Other families waiting to adopt from Romania couldn't now either. It was somewhat of an oxymoron. I saw hundreds of babies with my own eyes…so many of them. *Romanian government, what are you thinking?* I wasn't sure why Romania was doing this, but it didn't make sense. Even when international adoptions were open, thousands of babies still needed families.

Soon, news spread of why this was happening. Romania was not a part of the European Union at this time, and there were rumors that the adoption ban had something to do with that. I realized this later, but at the time, not very many Romanians adopted children. It wasn't just American's who were adopting, but people from all over Europe were adopting Romanian children. I believe the desire stemmed from communism being overthrown in Romania. People finally found out about the thousands and thousands of babies being institutionalized, malnourished and with almost no human contact. When people around the world heard about it, they started adopting Romanian babies. Sadly, this new law was going to prevent children from having the chance to have families.

I understand the process was not perfect, but precious lives were caught in limbo because of new changes. Romania was on the cusp of major change because they wanted to be a part of the European Union, and Casandra and I were caught in it. This was a vital time in this country's history. Other rumors spread as to why they closed the adoptions, but my thoughts still remained the same. Crack down on why women are abandoning their children here and you may find a far better solution than closing international adoptions.

The social worker shared with me on another occasion that there may be a chance to adopt her if I got a residency permit to stay in the country. She also shared with me that it was necessary to find Casandra's birth mother to start the process of classifying her as "officially abandoned." This would make her "adoptable." But there was a big problem...they didn't know where her birth mother was. During this conversation, the social worker looked in Casandra's records and found out that her birth mom was only 14 years old when she gave birth to her.

My mouth dropped in shock. That was so young! *Fourteen?* *She was just a baby herself.* I had a momentary glimpse of seeing myself at that altar after hearing Heidi Baker speak. My heart had no ill feelings for her anymore. I started to see that maybe she left Casandra in the best place she could have: at a hospital.

Chapter 14

A Friend of Orphans

It was summer now, and I took Casandra out to the courtyard for some fresh air. She had a tight little bonnet on her head that the nurses had put on. I went to untie the bonnet so the warm sun could shine on her face. As I was doing so, I heard a woman's voice from behind me.

"You shouldn't take that off her. Romanians believe that air can get into their ears and they will be sick. If they see you take it off, they will ask you to put it back on."

"Oh!" I responded as I stopped untying the ribbon.

I turned around and there was an American woman walking with a child. He was holding her hand and walking slowly, little step by little step.

"Hi, I'm Halie," I said, wondering why in the world a baby would need to wear such a headpiece in the hot weather with no wind blowing.

"I'm Dawn. How old do you think this boy is?"

I looked at the child she was helping to walk evaluated his height and body stature in mind and said, "Six?"

Dawn told me that he was almost 16. Come to find out this little guy, Sanyi, was put into the orphanage in 1988 when Romania was still a communist country. I had heard stories of how bad things were in the orphanages at that time. Dawn shared that he was basically confined to a crib his whole life. Before my eyes was a life and a body mangled from others' choices. It hurt my heart to see little Sanyi. I couldn't believe it, but I had to because he was standing there with his frail hand holding tight onto Dawn's.

Sanyi couldn't talk. Later, I found out he had Down Syndrome. He was very thin and saliva dripped out of the corner of his mouth. His conditions still didn't stop him from smiling. He still smiled, a lot! Dawn told me that his favorite thing was to crawl up on her lap in a rocking chair and to have her rock him. I looked at Dawn and admired her compassion and strong heart.

Because of my certainty, I shared with Dawn that I was going to adopt Casandra. She also shared her story with me. In our conversation, I found out she was a physical therapist from Arizona. She came to Romania specifically to work with disabled kids. We became friends that day.

As our friendship grew, we knew we could count on each other. Not only did Dawn take care of Sanyi, but she fell in love with a tiny baby girl named Mila. We would take these two to the therapist's room and have them play. We would blow bubbles and watch them track the bubbles with their eyes, fascinated as they floated in the air.

We had good days together loving these babies and we also had hard days. Dawn cared for the ones that no one cared for. She called me multiple times, crying and hurting, when a few of these children died. In one case, Dawn was the only one who showed up for an orphan's funeral. In America, the thought of that seems incomprehensible to have only one person come to a child's funeral. Dawn is a hero in the eyes of Jesus. I think Dawn lives sacrificially because she sees Jesus loving the least of these. They matter to her because she knows they matter to God.

Chapter 15

The Wolf

There was one morning, like most mornings, when I was in a hurry to see Casandra. Through the gate of the orphanage I went, through the building, around the corner to the stairs, and then a stranger stopped me. I had never seen him before, and was surprised when he spoke English (and sounded American). The conversation was disturbing.

"Are you the one allowed in the baby section?" He asked abruptly.

"Yeeeees," I answered slowly, still reeling from the shock of being stopped.

"Well, then what foundation are you with?"

"I'm not with any foundation."

The man became visibly upset and started to chuckle when I gave him the answer.

"Well, then how much did you *pay* them to be with the babies?" His voice was shifting to an unsettling tone.

"Huh? I didn't pay them a penny! I just asked if I could take care of a baby that I was taking care of at the hospital and they said yes!" My heart began to pound with pressure. I was disgusted that he would think I would pay a bribe.

As he chuckled, he said, "I have been here for years and they will not let me in the baby section, so you must have done something to let them allow you to go in there!"

"I'm sorry, but all I did was ask! I have a baby to take care of, so if you'll please excuse me, I have to go." I walked past him and up the stairs to see Casandra.

I couldn't help but be a little freaked out by this guy's suggestions. *Who is this guy? What's with the creepy questions?* My stomach churned with a bad feeling. In all honesty, I had no idea I was the only one besides paid caretakers allowed with the babies. They had made a special exception for me—only me—to take care of Casandra. At least one good thing came of that awkward conversation: a state of awe that God was really so good! God gave me such favor with this place. A sense that I had to stay away from this guy nudged me inside.

From then on, any chance he got he would taunt me. Sometimes, I accidently ran into him. Other times, he would intentionally stand at the gate with an orphan child waiting for me to show up. I couldn't get past him quick enough. I couldn't believe such a man could be playing with these orphans. *He should not be working with these vulnerable kids...*

Because I had such a strong, troubling discernment about him, I went to the director to share that I had a bad feeling about this guy. Sadness filled her face when I told her. She then told me there was one other person who had also shared this observation with her. "Yes," I restated, "I don't think he is up to any good..."

Every day I continued to take the tram across town to be with Casandra. Every day my baby girl was being raised in an orphanage, but I was with her. Every day, I also went to some office in the town to try to figure out how in the world Romania would let me adopt her. Every morning I woke up with the sense that *this could be the day God will do a miracle.* I had to. Every day I would sing songs of freedom over her. Every day I would fight the fear, the pain in my heart, the sorrow of injustice, the upset stomach, the bad dreams, the antagonistic guy, the language barrier. Every day I had to go back to my apartment without her. Every day I fought for this God-ordained plan for Casandra and me.

When I had to leave the orphanage in the evening, I would place her in her crib, kiss her and go out the door. It was the hardest thing I had to do, and I hated that moment every day. As I turned to go one day, for the first time she grabbed a hold of her crib rail to force her little body up. She stood up, reached her arms up to me and said, "Momma!" I gasped, my face lit up and my heart danced. That was the first time she called me Momma. I went back into her room and picked her up. That one word gave me more fighting power to endure. I stayed quite a bit longer with my treasure that night. It was so hard to leave her.

Casandra's first birthday was spent in a room in the orphanage. The director had allowed me to have a little birthday party with her with some special friends. It was the first time she had met all of them (except Lavi), but my friends sure knew all about her and were excited to be with us on her special day. What a blessing to be surrounded by these special people in Romania who believed she would be mine soon too. Gelu, with his new wife, Anca, were there. They had just gotten married and had returned home from their honeymoon that very day. Here we were, sitting at a table with small gifts and a cake, singing happy birthday to Casandra. "Happy birthday dear Casandra…" Even though it wasn't how I envisioned her first birthday, it was a blessing.

Not only was her first birthday spent in the orphanage, but her first of many things. Her first words, the first time she sat up, her first steps. It was all-glorious, yet there was something unfulfilled. It was all-wonderful, but there was no answer. I kept telling myself *all that matters is that we are together for these milestones.* I tried my best not to wonder what was happening when I wasn't there. I tried my best not to imagine her crying in the night for me and not being there. I had to stop my thoughts in their tracks or else I would be on the border of depression.

Since Romania was in such a huge transition with new laws, not very many people knew what I had to do. I was trying to figure out how to get that permit to stay. I already had a visa stating that I was allowed to be there, but what I needed was different. What I needed was equivalent to an American green card. After many trips to the police station, I finally had some answers. They told me that in order to receive my "green card," I would have to stay in the country for five years without leaving. At that time, I had been in the country for less than a year without leaving. I was going to be here for much longer than I anticipated. Five years was a long time, but it didn't even matter to me how long I needed to stay in Romania. What did matter to me was Casandra getting out of the orphanage so that the rest of her 'first times' for things would be experienced in freedom.

Chapter 16

Eyes to Not See

One day on my usual route to Casandra's room, I was stopped by the social worker. She said that there had been a foundation there looking for babies to put into their foundation and they wanted Casandra to be one of them. I immediately reminded myself that God was in control and this may actually be a blessing for us. *Maybe I could be her foster parent for now?* I spoke with the director and she explained the name of the foundation and where it was. She drew a small map for me, and it dawned on me that it was the same foundation where Mabel worked. She was the lady who let me know what kind of papers I needed and so forth to adopt Casandra. I had spoken with her a few times and we occasionally corresponded with email. She knew of my intent to adopt Casandra, so my immediate thought was *Mabel can help us. Maybe she can take Casandra so we can have a better chance of legalizing the adoption.*

Later on that evening, I called her to confirm that she was helping us.

"Hi Mabel! I heard that you were at the orphanage and they told me that you want to take Casandra?"

She rudely responded, "What did you think, she was going to stay in the orphanage her whole life?"

"No, of course not. That is why I came for her. That is why I told you I was going to adopt her."

"Well, we have plans for her."

"Why would you do that when you know I came back for her? I am going to adopt her."

I can't quite remember how that conversation ended, but I remember what I did and how I felt: I felt betrayed. And by a fellow American, no less! Once again, I fell to my knees. I cried out to God. After that prayer, I felt that things were still going to work out for us. Even if she put Casandra into this foundation for a time, I was still going to adopt her! From the depths of my heart, I cried out to God and told Him, "I trust You, God! I trust You, God!"

Despite my declaration of trust, it had been another concern, another weight set on my heart. My body ached. I typically couldn't sleep very well anyway, but this night was worse. Through the tossing and turning, I was holding onto His voice.

Upon my arrival to see Casandra the next day, the social worker was passing through the outside walkway. When she spotted me, she came to me with boldness and this is what she said:

"Halie, you came for this girl. You came and you are going to adopt her. It is my decision where Casandra goes and she is not going anywhere without you. She will stay here until she gets to come out with you!"

I burst into tears and leapt to hug her tight around the neck. My lips could not stop thanking her. When I turned to go see my baby, I knew that God had spoken. He had spoken, and put that decision in her heart! There was no need to convince her that Casandra was my baby. God was there with us!

Again, I am reminded of the word of God. He tells us to be strong and courageous. He tells us to cast our cares upon Him because He cares for us. This is a perfect example of when we are weak, He is strong. I could do my small piece, and He had to do the impossible. I was fighting my battle through prayers because this battle belonged to Him.

I didn't write about Mabel and her "other plans for Casandra" to shame her. What she did to me really stinks; it was like a knife to my back. I thought she was someone on our team, but she was just another "naysayer." Someone else I knew while living there told me that Mabel had told her *there was no way Halie would adopt Casandra*. Whenever God has big plans for someone, there's always a naysayer. There always is one, or maybe two or ten people who just don't understand. It may not even be for them to understand *your* purpose. I just had to keep in mind that God was a "Yes-sayer" on this one. Because of this lady's ignorance, I got to see another miracle performed by my Daddy in Heaven. I forgave her and actually am glad our story gets to be that much more amazing because of what she tried to do! Maybe

God didn't give Mabel eyes to see this adoption finalized, but I had them. He wanted my faith to endure through this bump in the road.

The social worker at the orphanage started to look for Casandra's birth mother again. She sent a letter to the last location where they knew she had been: the village her birth mother was from. It went to the police station in the village. From there, the police would try to locate her and send in the response. The response came back one day through the mail system. She was not at this village. The search continued.

Chapter 17

Miracle Home

Day in and day out at the orphanage, things continued to trail on with my baby girl. Seasons changed and soon it was rounding to winter again. Knowing that I had to get a home study done, I was nervous about bringing a social worker to my apartment that was gradually falling apart. I didn't think it was a home they would approve bringing a baby home to.

To my knees I went. For my morning prayers, I added, "Please, God, provide a new home I can bring Casandra to when she is able to leave the orphanage." It didn't take long for God to answer this prayer.

Standing at the trolley station waiting for my trolley in the morning, I looked around at the beautiful culture of Romania. The ladies sold flowers every morning in front of a little orthodox church. Watching the people stop to get a fresh loaf of uncut bread at the bakery. The crosswalks were full of people walking to work. Glancing around, I noticed a lady also waiting for a trolley.

She had blonde hair and was wearing American brand quality clothes. Immediately I could tell she was American!

I wasn't shy and went straight to her to introduce myself. Her name was Liz and it was nice meeting her and hearing about what she was doing in Romania. She told me that she was teaching Bible classes at a church she was attending there, and I exchanged my reason for being in Romania.

We boarded the same trolley since we were headed to the same part of town. We sat near each other conversing and answering each of our intriguing questions about one another. Then Liz asked me if I was looking for an apartment to move into. *Why yes, yes I am!*

Liz explained that she was going back to the states soon and wanted to find someone to move in since she put a lot of love into her apartment. She also mentioned she would even sell some items very inexpensively to me. That made me happy, since I didn't own any furniture yet. It was glorious to hear that her apartment was just down the street from where I was living now and even closer to the trolley station. I loved that it was in the same neighborhood. We decided I would go visit the apartment the following morning to see what I thought.

The next day before I headed over to see her apartment, I prayed…

"God, I want to move there if it's where You want me to live, but it may be really nice and not where You want me to live. Is this apartment mine?" Gently, I heard the Lord say, "It is yours."

Some might think this is weird, but my heart is to just be where He wants me. It means a lot to make the best decisions for my life, because God knows what's best for us. I just love how if it matters to us, so it must matter to Him.

I'm pretty certain that I skipped down the road to the address Liz gave me. There was an intercom at the door, and I rang the apartment number to hear Liz's voice. She buzzed me in, reminding me she was on the eighth floor. The elevator took me up and I knocked on my future door. Liz opened and my eyes were happy. This apartment was amazing! It was three bedrooms with two baths. No tile was falling off anywhere. It had two balconies. One looked out to the country where houses were being built, and one was directly facing the city where Romanian, busy life was happening. It was beautiful.

"Well, do you like it?" Liz asked after she gave me the tour.

"Oh yes! I love it!"

God had ordained my steps again. Liz and I had lived so close to each other for months and never saw a glimpse of one another, not one time. This was a home I did want to take Casandra home to. Another real miracle was that it was only $40 more a month than where I was currently living. What a blessing! There was another weight off of my shoulders.

After I saw my new home, I carried on to the orphanage. You better believe that I picked Casandra up and twirled her around with the news of our news home. I told her all about it.

A few days later, I was already settled into our new, beautiful home. Before Liz had left, she found an adorable white, wooden crib for Casandra. I put it together the first chance I had! It was such a sweet gesture from her to get for us. It was also telling me she believed the adoption was going to happen and that God will provide for us. Every bit of encouragement, I happily took.

Chapter 18

First Visit Out

Christmas was approaching and I desperately wanted to celebrate with Casandra out of the orphanage. I asked the director if there was a way I could bring her home with me for a few days. She said I would need to get approval by the head director over the country's orphanages. If I got the approval I could. Thankfully, his office was in the same town I lived in. She helped me with writing the letter and I prayed. I had already been down in the dumps for some time with constant bad news and I needed a break. *Please, God. Help this work out...*

I went to the office to meet with the director as boldly as I could. He read the letter, read over my home study and asked a few questions. I prayed in my mind as he analyzed the situation. This was the first time I was able to share with him about our story. He listened intently. It was hard to read what he was thinking from his stoic posture. Finally, he agreed that she could come out of the orphanage for a visit. My excitement was hard to contain!

It was going to be Casandra's first time out in the real world, *ever*! What a treat! I started buying gifts and preparing our first Christmas together. It was also going to be my first Christmas away from my family. It was a Christmas that forged our own traditions. Freedom was a tradition we never want to take for granted.

I have the sweetest memories the day I brought Casandra home to our apartment. The first thing I did was make her a warm bath with bubbles. My eyes just stared at her little, wet hands. There were those fascinating bubbles again, as suds covered the top of the water in her baby basin. It was so cute; she didn't know what to do with them. She gently patted her hand on the top to touch the white suds. Then she would look up at me and pat some more. She loved it, and she smiled a big, amused smile. It was her first time taking a bubble bath, and my heart was determined to have her experience all of what a one-year-old could in four short days.

Our first night home, I cuddled her tight. When morning broke, we both woke up at the same time. My head started to face towards her and she said with a huge smile on her face, "Hiiiiii, Momma!" I looked at her big brown eyes locked on mine and said, "Hiiiii, Momma's Baby."

Oh, what a beautiful morning!

I made sure to make Christmas calls to Grandpa, Grandma, Uncle and Auntie so she could hear their voices. To them it felt like answers. A while back, I had made a little photo book and put all of their pictures in it. Each day I showed it to her, naming each person as we looked at it. She loved to stare particularly at my nephew, her cousin. They were only two months apart, and I would also dream of the cousin memories they would make together someday.

We didn't go outside much because of the blistering cold weather, but I did bundle her up and make it to church for a Christmas service. My friends who had been praying for her were delighted to see her. The night before Christmas it had snowed. This meant that we both got to experience our first white Christmas together! I had her presents wrapped and it was fun showing her the surprises under the pretty wrapping paper. For most of Christmas Day it was just the two of us. We did get a special visit from Lavi, and the three-of-us just enjoyed celebrating our Savior's birth together in Romania.

It was the normal, everyday moments with Casandra that I enjoyed most in our apartment. I enjoyed watching her try to walk back and forth in the living room. She was 14 months now and had not got walking completely under control. She walked a few steps and grabbed the coffee table, and a few more to reach the sofa. I enjoyed making her food, getting her dressed and making sure she had a clean diaper every time she needed a new one. We enjoyed the bedtime books and morning cuddles. Even combing out her wet hair after the bath and blow-drying it were moments I cherished. We didn't have most of those luxuries while she was still in the orphanage. I was so happy to have her in our home.

It was awful bringing Casandra back to the orphanage after our four-day break together. It hurt so badly. I had to take her back. Wanting to capture every spare moment, I waited until the evening to call a cab. We pulled up and the knot grew. Those were the hardest steps, walking her back into that orphanage. She had to know that it was going to be okay though. I held myself together even though I wanted to fall apart.

By that time, the ladies who worked at the orphanage had become our friends, and they missed us for those few days we were gone. That made it better. It made it better knowing a few of them missed seeing Casandra even though they were glad she was with me. I took her to her room and held her tight. I sang, "Where the Spirit of the Lord is there is freedom" until she fell asleep. I laid down and kissed her check before my tears could wake her up.

Day in and day out, the weeks and months dragged on. I continued to sing those songs of freedom, dismissing my stomach aches. My body became tired, but my will was strong. My strength was in Jesus alone. I had to rely on Him to get to her every day. I had to rely on Him to leave her every evening in the safety of His hands, trusting that no harm would befall her while I was not by her side.

One glimpse of fresh breath was my best friend, Crystal, who had decided to come back to Romania to also adopt. There was a little boy, Gabriel, who she cared for in the hospital. God was tugging on her heart to do the same. Once you are exposed to the need, it's hard to turn a blind eye to it. Crystal has a heart of gold and a heart to love orphans. How could she not come back? The timing was perfect because my heart was aching after taking Casandra back after Christmas.

My best friend and I would wake up in the morning and head out to our babies. Her stop was before mine at a foundation where her precious Gabriel was now, and my stop was a few after that. At the day's end when we would come home, we would tell stories of what Casandra and Gabriel did that day. Our stories ranged from what they ate to the new words they learned that day. While we were not with them, we were talking about them nonstop. It was just two mommas talking about their babies.

I still needed answers. I still needed to know how in the world this adoption was going to work. *God, please send me someone who knows what they are doing and has real answers. I need someone who knows how to do this.* It had to be someone who knew the laws; someone who could tell me this was going to happen. Anything.

Casandra fell asleep in my arms for her nap, and I sat down and stared at her like I usually would. We were tucked in the last room down the hall at the orphanage. This room had a mattress on the floor where we would play. I would massage her tiny little legs and arms and pray for strength and joy over her as she slept.

All of a sudden, I heard voices down the hall. Little pitter-patter feet were running my way. Those little feet made their way to the door of our room, and peeked in was a toddler boy. Then, I noticed those voices I heard were not in Romanian, they were in English. I peered out from the room to see a girl about my age with the director. She had a man with her with a camera and the little boy was with them.

We introduced ourselves. Her name was Sandra and she was from England. Come to find out, her little boy was also at that orphanage before. She had started a foundation for orphans in Romania and was also trying to adopt this little boy. She assured me that she was working on him getting adopted as well. The man who was with her was a reporter also from England. He was apparently there to do a story on her and what she was doing in Romania. That is the reason they came to the orphanage. He snapped a few pictures, but the director had to remind him that he was not allowed to take any.

The reporter wanted to see where her little guy was before he was with Sandra. Their visit was a ray of sunlight to me. God was being so faithful in answering my prayers. It felt good to know someone else was in my same boat! What a relief! Sandra and I exchanged numbers and she gave me information to a foundation that may be able to help.

Very quickly I got in contact with this foundation on the phone. I called right after Sandra left, while Casandra was still sleeping. It was music to my ears, when the director agreed to meet with me the following day.

During the meeting, I found out that this foundation had children under their care and then put into families to be taken care of instead of in the orphanage. They had agreed to help me first look for Casandra's birth mother. I retold the steps we had already taken to find her birth mom, and they wanted to take a more aggressive approach: to physically drive to a village she may have been.

As you read this you may be thinking driving to a town and just asking around for someone is silly. It's not like going to a town in the US though. First of all, Romania is about the size of Oregon. Within the nation, there are little villages. Some villages have mostly gypsies, officially called Roma people, living in them. Since Casandra was gypsy descent, it narrowed our search.

Two social workers and an eager mom in a Romanian-brand Dacia car, headed to a village where Casandra's mom could possibly be. We pulled up on the dirt road that had just been wet from the rain to a group of girls. These girls, olive tone skin, dressed in long skirts had muddy feet from the rain. They had allowed the car to pull up next to them. The social worker who was driving rolled down his window to ask if they knew Casandra's birth mom. The girls responded that they knew who she was, but they said she didn't live there anymore. They also didn't know where she was. The social worker then asked if they knew anything about her birth mother's family. They shared with us that they knew the mom's mom had died a few years back, but that was all they knew. This was all the investigating we did for the day. It was little progress, but it felt good to be doing something proactive.

On the way back to town, my mind started racing. I had just found out that Casandra's birth mother was possibly alone. Maybe that was another possible reason she didn't keep Casandra. During some small talk with the social workers in the car, they told me finding Casandra's birth mother was vital to get her under their foundation. There was nothing they could do until they found her.

I ended up feeling very frustrated because nothing was happening. I thought God had sent them to me to help, yet their hands were tied. The only thing we knew was that her birth mom was not in this tiny village. We had the rest of Romania to search through. My ray of hope dimmed. During the moment of disappointment, ironically it started to rain on the way back to Oradea. The sky was gray. It was the deepest gray I had ever seen. Finally, forward movement came and I found someone to help, but no. Never mind. The help turned out to make me feel utter despair. One tiny pebble was unturned in a vast valley of pebbles. *How many more pebbles need to be unturned with the right answer lying underneath it?*

From my point of view, because Casandra was already 18 months old, why did we even have to find her birth mother? After we find her, we have to have enough faith to believe she will actually sign the papers to officially abandon her. It was so unjust to me. After this long, the child's case should be on to the next step. Of course, I thought about Casandra the most, but what about every other child I saw at the orphanage? How long did they have to wait to be officially abandoned? I was the one fighting for her, but did the other babies have someone to fight for them? This is one reason why I spent many nights crying and praying for all the abandoned babies of Romania. There were laws prohibiting these children to be adopted. The injustice of it all was painful to watch, and I had a front row seat.

After the visit to the first village day, I asked this foundation what else we could do. I tried to pry for more help, but everyone had his or her own caseload to work through. My case was not a priority for anyone there. I didn't understand why it wasn't working out. No one called me, no one had another plan and there was no effort put forward to help us.

Soon it was Easter, and I did the same thing I had done for Christmas to hopefully get Casandra out for a couple of days. I wrote a letter, got it approved and started preparing Easter for us. I came to the orphanage that day like the Easter bunny…hopping with happiness. I entered the building and went upstairs to get my baby girl. The lady director who had helped me so much went on maternity leave and the director in her place wanted to speak to me. When I walked into her office, she gave me bad news. There was a baby who ended up with the chicken pox and the whole orphanage was quarantined. I didn't even know what that meant at the time, but she explained to me that Casandra could not leave. Oh, how I was crushed!

Crystal had also asked if she may spend time with Gabriel in our apartment for Easter. She got the approval for Easter day, but this meant we still had to spend it away from each other. Our babies wouldn't be able to see each other and play together again. I was happy for her. It was different spending time with Casandra in our apartment, and I was so glad she got to experience that with Gabriel.

I was heartbroken because Casandra could not come home this time though. I still was determined to celebrate our first Easter together. Crystal and I had dyed Easter eggs for Gabriel and Casandra. They were still babies, but we thought we could still start our Easter traditions with them. We prepared some yummy food and picked out cute outfits for them to wear.

This particular Easter in Romania was cold and rainy. I went to church. During the service, they mentioned that there would be a couple from America speaking later. I had no intention of going because I planned on spending the whole day after church with Casandra. I took a mental note that *I will not be attending that*, then the Holy Spirit said, "I want you to go." I argued back that I didn't want to go. Then Holy Spirit said, "I'm going to speak to you there." I grumbled with God, not wanting to go, but told Him that I would go if He wanted me to. I was still upset about not being able to take Casandra home and took it out on God.

As soon as the morning Easter service was over, I headed out to the orphanage. Casandra was eating her lunch when I arrived, so I took over for one of the nurses. After she ate, I dressed her in a cute dress my grandma had sent over for her. I hid the eggs down the hall and walked her through finding them and placing them in her Easter basket. It was fun and she finally caught onto it. I stayed until dark that evening. I didn't want to leave her. She should have been home with me.

When I could muster up the strength to actually leave, I remembered about the church service the Holy Spirit told me to go to. I just wanted to go home, hear how Crystal's day was with Gabriel and go to sleep so the next day could come all the sooner and once again I would be with my baby. On the way to the tram, I got wet from the rain. My feet squished through the mud puddles down the path on the dirt road to the church. I was late and wet, but I snuck in and sat in the back. Honestly, I was quite grumpy. I just wanted Casandra home, but here I was wet and at church because God told me to go.

The speakers, a couple from the States, had very prophetic giftings. They were praying for people and I sat there, sad; sad I didn't have my baby out yet. Soon, the lady speaking pointed at me. "You, the girl with the striped shirt. Come forward." I looked down at my shirt and yep, it was striped. She was talking about me. I slowly went to the front, hoping people wouldn't notice how much of a mess I was, inside and out.

The woman started to pray for me. I must have done a great job blending with the Romanians, since I think she thought I was Romanian. She told me some powerful words and prayed for me. She didn't mention anything to do with Casandra, but it still encouraged me. God called me out that night to encourage me, since I was down and out. Through that, He reminded me that I did hear His voice once again.

Before this chicken pox Easter incident, I seemed to withstand anything that came my way. God had given me a supernatural strength to battle the hits. The hope of having her home with me again and then to be disappointed was devastating. I had to remind myself that God sees me; God sees all of this mess. I actually took comfort in Him knowing the ins and outs. There was someone who knew really what I was going through.

For a whole month, chicken pox was passed from baby to baby, but the virus did not reach Casandra, ever. The quarantine lasted that entire time, and during this, they would not even let me take her outside for fresh air. She and I had to stay in the little room where her crib was. Despite everything going on, Casandra had the biggest smile on her face most of the time. For me though, the orphanage became darker. The smell became stronger. The pain became unbearable. Weariness was setting in.

Chapter 19

On Earth as it is in Heaven

Before I went to see Casandra one morning, I was in my room praying. My heart ached with the longing to enjoy a normal life with my baby. I called out to God like I did every day, but today the call was deeper. During my time talking with Jesus, I saw a short vision that helped my faith. In my mind's eye, I saw a beautiful angel carrying a document. When the angel got closer, I was able to see it was Casandra's birth certificate. It had her name on it and my name as her mother. Then, the angel brought the bottom section to my attention. That portion of the birth certificate got larger. It was signed by Jesus. Not only was it signed by Jesus, but it was signed in the color red, which I understood to mean it was signed in His blood.

The presence of God in my room was so strong, and I immediately knew what the vision it meant. The Lord showed me that it is finished in Heaven. In Heaven, she was mine and the document was finalized in the blood of Jesus. That meant absolutely nothing could stop it. From that day on, my prayers changed. Instead of begging God to make things happen, to please make her mine, anxiously crying out for Him to do something, I realized He had *already* done it. I started to pray, "His Kingdom come, His will be done, on Earth as it is in Heaven." If it was complete in Heaven, on Earth was next.

After that vision, I knew in Heaven that it was done, but it was my responsibility to pray what was already in Heaven to Earth. That's how Jesus told us to pray. Because God had so graciously showed me this during my time with Him, a refreshed faith grew in my heart. The impossible didn't seem too big of a mountain in front of me. This was His will for me; this was His will for Casandra.

This moment I had wasn't weird. The scene I saw floated around vividly in my imagination. Someone once explained to me God created that part of us. He created our imagination to be a place where God, Jesus and the Holy Spirit can speak to us. It's like God beautifies our imagination and shows us what He is thinking about in situations when we really need it.

Both Crystal and I always knew that we needed a miracle to happen for Casandra to get out. The pain got to a point that I couldn't take it anymore. That's when Crystal and I decided to knock on Heaven's door a little *louder*. For a month, we decided we would do the Daniel fast. In the Bible, Daniel had eaten a certain way, causing him to grow stronger. The Daniel fast is all about eating only vegetables (read more about this in Daniel 10:12). We were okay with also adding fruit to our fast. We would do it while steadfastly praying for Casandra to be able to come out of the orphanage.

Oh, Crystal and I were a hoot trying to figure out new things to eat that only contained fruits and vegetables for 30 days! We had to change our way of eating, that's for sure! One fun thing we did was to freeze fruit for our evening snack. Before we froze the fruit, we stuck toothpicks in them. While on our way to see our babies, we made special trips to the only health food store in our town to get banana chips. It was hard, but we both stayed faithful to how God was leading us to pray. We lost a few pounds during the month, but gained a lot of energy! We seemed to be hungry all of the time though…

Crystal also needed a miracle for Gabriel. It wasn't long before a family was interested in adopting him. Gabriel had blue eyes, blonde hair and an adorable smile. He was starting to walk and talk and became quite healthy. His once skinny little arms were now plump. The director of the foundation Gabriel was under had a tough decision to make. She eventually made the decision for this family to adopt him. I believe she made that decision because Crystal seemed to be so far away from getting her "green card."

Crystal had to endure the visits when they came to see him before they could take him home. She would come back from the apartment emotionally drained. We would pray, cry a little and believe God knew best. The director decided that Crystal would be the one to take him to his new family. Usually the social worker or another worker from the same orphanage would take a child to their new home for the first time, but this director saw fit that Crystal would be the one to take him. Gabriel knew Crystal the best. Crystal wanted my support and asked if I was able to come with her.

Finding the perfect words for this part of the story and the night when we dropped Gabriel off might not be possible. Gabriel was chosen by new parents. Crystal cared for him when he was skin and bones. The baby who she cared for with every fiber of her being was just like I cared for Casandra. The baby that would have been left alone for hours upon hours had a momma to pray over him and care for him. The time was not wasted. The time was well spent. However, the time didn't last long enough.

We had to spend the night in Gabriel's new home and head back to town the next day. There was such awkwardness between this family and us. It wasn't personal. They were nice. They were probably going to be amazing parents, but my best friend was in so much pain. We had only what seemed a few minutes with Gabriel before it was time to turn out the lights for bed.

Crystal couldn't go to sleep and was basically sick to her stomach from losing him. It didn't help that we could hear him crying in the other room. This place was new to him and his cry from the hall made Crystal's heart pinch into a tiny ball. It took everything in her to not go and comfort him. I tried my best to comfort her. Then I just knelt on the side of her bed and prayed. I prayed over Crystal and prayed for her heart. I prayed until I heard her sound asleep. I got off of my knees in the dark and crawled into bed.

I laid there past midnight and thought of Casandra. This was the last day of our month-long fast. Crystal and I didn't talk about our last few fasting days before this. How could I bring things up? How could I even talk about Casandra after she just went through this pain of losing Gabriel? We were so focused on Gabriel leaving that we didn't talk much about our fast being over. We just knew it was over.

We woke up the next day, gathered our things and Gabriel's new dad was quick to drop us off at the train station. My eyes were so blurry with water ready to explode from them as I gave Gabriel one last hug. I started for the car to let Crystal tell him bye. I was a mess, but had to be strong for her. She walked to him and gave him a hug that would hold all of the stars in the sky.

We got into the car and drove off to the train station and soon boarded our train. Neither of us said a word. What could I possibly say to make her heart not break?

There wasn't anything to say to her; I just sat next to her. My words would have fallen short of easing the pain. I remember thinking about Casandra and how I couldn't wait to see her. That's how I felt every morning when I woke up, but at that moment I felt selfish and guilty about thinking about it. I just stared out of the window at the sunflower fields of Romania as the train tugged us along.

We were halfway back to our town, and Crystal broke the silence.

"I'm so glad our girl is coming home today!" She said as she glanced towards me.

That was our plan: to pray, to fast, to go with boldness and beg for her release. My best friend, in the midst of her brokenness had enough courage to still have hope for me; hope that Casandra was coming home that day! I looked at her and smiled.

The train reached Oradea and we took a taxi to our apartment. We went in and I went straight for Casandra's diaper bag to head out to get her. I remember feeling bad for leaving my best friend in such a sad state, but I knew she understood. Since taking a taxi was the fastest way to get to the orphanage, I called one right away. When I got there, I ran up the stairs to her room, dressed her into a cute little outfit, put her on my hip and headed down the stairs again.

It was another absolute miracle that the head director of the county was there at the orphanage that day. He was the one who approved or denied requests like these. He was the one who had allowed me to take her home for Christmas and had approved my Easter request as well. As I headed for the office door to meet with him, at the same moment, he came out of the door briskly to leave. I stopped him and in my best broken Romanian, pleaded that she come home with me. He recognized me from my many visits to his office to try to find answers. I told him I had been working on getting my permit to stay. I told him that my home study was already complete (in order to have her in my home) and reminded him of how dedicated I had been every day to come take care of her. Then I told him about the darn chicken pox and how she couldn't even leave her room. "Please, it isn't fair for her to be here anymore when she has someone to take care of her." Casandra was already 20 months and I couldn't bear her growing up in the orphanage any longer.

He listened to me. Even though he was in a rush, he truly listened to every word I said. He looked at the psychologist who worked there and who was standing next to me. He asked her if I was there every day. She agreed and said, adamantly, "EVERY DAY!" She put such urgency in her voice when she replied.

The chief director looked back at me with an unsteady look and said, "I am very busy today. Come to my office next week."

Oh no…it was Friday! I couldn't go another day.

Out of my mouth came these desperate words, "Please, no! Please let her come out today!"

After all, God had already done miracle after miracle. I was in a spot where I couldn't take no for an answer anymore. He looked and looked at Casandra and said:

"Okay, I will sign a release for her to live with you."

The psychologist at the orphanage took a paper and wrote swiftly a letter of release and he signed it.

A miracle! My heart burst with joy. The director signed a paper, and then I signed it too. Quicker than quick I was out the door with her in my arms. Casandra was still on my hip when the psychologist called a taxi for me. Everyone who was there witnessing this beamed with joy! They were happy for us.

I flew out of the orphanage as quick as I could before anyone could change his or her minds. The taxi came and I gave the driver our address. We got in and I was homeward bound with my Casandra. *This is actually happening!* My face was smiling and my heart was smiling even more. There was still a layer of dried tears on my face from a few hours earlier when my best friend lost Gabriel.

Back then, Romania didn't have seat belt laws for people riding in the back seat. I held her tight on my lap, wrapping my arms around her, and whispered, "We are going home!" When I got to the apartment, I threw money at the driver and walked with her in my arms to the elevator. The elevator couldn't move fast enough to the eighth. I unlocked our apartment door and heard Crystal in the living room.

"You are back already?" Crystal asked, as her voice trailed down the long hall.

"Yeah, they wouldn't let me see her!" I said jokingly as I rushed to her.

Crystal was sitting on the couch in a ball, wrapped in a blanket with wet tissues all over. As I stepped in with Casandra on my hip, it's like the couch had an ejector seat. She exploded off the couch, grabbed Casandra and started jumping up and down saying, "I knew she was coming home today! I knew she was coming home today!"

I tell you what, there could have not been a better day for Casandra to come out of the orphanage. It could have happened any morning, but God choose this one to pour joy into our mourning. As I look back while I write this, I see how God chose this day from the beginning of the story. He loves Casandra, yes, and He also loves Crystal.

Was all the endurance needed up 'til now pointing to *this* day? Was it ALL for this one day? It most definitely was.

The next couple of days were spent enjoying Casandra in her new surroundings. We took her to the park, let her eat ice cream and had so much fun teaching her new things. My family back home was thrilled to hear the news and started planning trips to come and see us. My dad, my sister, my mom, my Aunt, even my grandma made plans! A huge step was accomplished, but the road was not close to being over. As long as I didn't have to leave her ever again in the orphanage, it didn't really matter to me.

Crystal left ten days after Casandra came home. She felt it was time for her to return to the States. I wanted her to stay, but I understood. At every turn here she would think of Gabriel. Not only that, but the mission God had set before her in Romania had ended. She put all of her heart into loving Gabriel while she was there.

Before she left, I had a dream one night. In the dream, a little boy about eight years old was coming down the stairs at my dad's house. He looked up at me and said, "Hi, Auntie!" I told Crystal the dream and told her that I thought for sure it was Gabriel. He had blonde hair and bright, light eyes. Little did I know that she would tuck this dream in her heart and still wonder if it meant anything.

Chapter 20

Social Worker Angel

Casandra was home to enjoy all of those sweet freedoms again with me, but the adoption process still had a lot to be accomplished. She was still officially under the administration of this particular orphanage, even though she was home. I was not comfortable with that at all, but the situation was much better now that she was home. No more leaving her every evening, and we were bonding like never before.

In the meantime, almost every second of the day she was by my side. I didn't miss the bath times anymore. I didn't miss the meal times anymore. I didn't miss the sweet dream times either. She was with me. Every time she cried, which wasn't very often, I was there. Every time she giggled, my ears were there to catch the sound. She was by my side, on my hip and always put to sleep in my arms.

Her crib was at the end of my bed. Even though she had her own room, I wanted her close to me. It only took a few nights for her to figure out how to get out of her crib and crawl in my bed. I would wake up with her next to me every morning. This child had my heart.

The very freedom from the orphanage's four walls made for many new things for her to experience. Whether it was running through a pile of leaves on a walk or petting a dog that walked by, she constantly had a smile on her face. There were so many new things to see, and it seemed like she was on a mission to see it all…and quickly.

Because it wasn't working with that one foundation that initially tried to help me, I knew I had to move on and find another solution. Unfortunately, the foundation that started to help find her birth mom was too busy doing their own caseload. I was okay with that, but it meant God needed to send plan B my way. Once again, I prayed my heart out for God to bring someone my way who knew what in the world to do. My mission was not complete and I still needed a lot of answers.

Through a series of meeting different people, about a year later God led me to a foundation called People to People. The director agreed to meet with me. I shared our story with him and he instantly said that he would help me. It was different from the other ones. I could tell this guy was one to work hard for these kids in Romania.

The director had several social workers who helped his foundation and he assigned one to work with my case. He introduced me to Ciprian, and he gave him the full green light to help us.

We still had no clue where Casandra's birth mom was, so it became Ciprian's mission to find her. He went out one day, village to village, to search. Evening came, and I got a call from him. No luck. He didn't find her. In my own mind, it stirred up the holy anger about this policy. Casandra was already three years old and the birth mom was nowhere to be found. It was quite ridiculous to have to wait and search for so long for someone when children should just be considered officially abandoned at some point so they can be adopted.

Ciprian still didn't give up hope. He reassured me he would find her. My last situation with the other foundation made my heart wonder constantly if they were serious about helping. But Ciprian looked at it differently. Some time later, He decided to go out another day to different places to find her. Again, at the end of the day I got a call from him.

"Halie, we went to some villages and could not find her. Then it started to snow, and I thought *come on let's go to one more village*. And GUESS WHAT?! We FOUND her! Halie, we found her and she signed the papers!"

Standing in the hall of my apartment on the phone, I just started to cry. I fell to my knees and thanked God. This time my cry was in relief and thankfulness. I then repeatedly thanked Ciprian. He had so much excitement in his voice when he told me. Finally, someone cares! There was a true human being who was fighting for us. I got off the phone with him and I remember picking Casandra up in my arms and swinging her around. She didn't know why mommy was being silly and crying at the same time. She just enjoyed the moment and giggled!

What a relief! We were another huge step closer. That day, Ciprian officially became my angel who God had sent to

Casandra and me. I assured Ciprian that God had send him to help us. This was a miracle! I don't think he truly understood what a blessing he was to us. For all of those years of having no one to help us, we had someone and now we actually had a signature!

Ciprian had to take the birth mom to a notary in the town where they found her to get these papers officially signed. Thank God she had identification. The sad thing was she could barely write her name because of how uneducated she was. I hounded Ciprian with questions about what she looked like and how she was. All he could tell me was that she was "absolutely beautiful." They had to make a copy of her ID card and attach it to the papers. I got the chance to see them. It was in black and white ink and the copy wasn't clear to see any resemblances that Casandra may have. I had my own idea of what her birth mother could look like. But this was what I had to make the mystery of her not so mysterious anymore.

Now that we knew where Casandra's birth mom was, I asked Ciprian if there was any way to bring Casandra to the States with me for a visit. It had been almost three years since I had stepped foot onto American soil. I missed my family. I wanted Casandra to grow up knowing her cousins, aunties, uncles and grandparents. A break for me from living overseas for so long would be good. Ciprian explained to me that it was possible. This man not only found out that it was possible, but figured out what we needed to do to make a trip home happen.

We needed four things to accomplish this: another paper signed by her birth mother, approval by the committee at the orphanage, get her passport and a trip to the American Embassy in Bucharest for another approval to get a visa for her to come. The first two things got accomplished quite quickly, but how in the world was my country going to approve a little child's "visit" with me to America? I wasn't sure how to tell the embassy my plan was adoption, since adoption of Romanian babies were still forbidden to any other country. I was also still very young and very single. I didn't know what they would think.

Ciprian wrote a paper up for Casandra's birth mom to sign. He went to see her again and asked if she would sign it. She agreed. The process of officially abandoning Casandra had not completely gone through the courts yet. That is why we still had to get a document from her birth mom. Again, it boggles me that birth mothers in cases like this still had power of attorney for their birth children. Casandra was going on four years old now. The paper he had her sign also stated that we could get Casandra her passport. Ciprian took her to the notary again to have the paper notarized. During this trip, he asked her if she ever tried to come back to visit Casandra when she was a baby. She told him that she had thought about it, but never actually attempted it.

Ciprian gathered other documents from the foundation to set before the child protection committee. I wasn't there when meeting time came, but I was praying while it was going on.

Ciprian, my angel, was at our defense. He told me about stating our case and basically reassured them I would responsibly take care of Casandra during our visit to the States. Since Ciprian had carefully aligned every piece of paperwork up, they agreed to allow her to come with me for a visit. He shared with me that a few people on the committee were uncertain, but he went to bat for us. He didn't just let them say no, he explained the love I have for Casandra and how he trusted me to take her for a visit. With his passion, they approved it!

Now that we had that approval, I was able to take Casandra to get her first passport. In Romania, the police station is where you file to get your passport. The police station seemed to take care of most of the nation's affairs. It was neat to bring her with me, because the officer who I always ran into was finally able to see Casandra. I think he was able to have a better idea as to why I needed my permit to stay in Romania. We had to wait a month for the passport to come. Once it came, we were able to make an appointment to the American Embassy.

Three steps down, and one more to go. My faith had been growing stronger and secure. By the time I had an appointment to the embassy, I started to pray a prayer like I had in the orphanage. God was being faithful to me. To show Him how much I believed the American Embassy was going to approve her visa home with me for a visit, I had so much faith that I just went ahead and bought our plane tickets.

Before I left Romania, I had a little savings account that I put money into for when I was a nanny. I didn't know what I was saving for at the time, but it makes me giggle how the money was for our plane tickets. It was the easiest, biggest purchase I had ever made. I was walking by faith once again in every detail of this story.

It was time to take a train to the capital of Romania. The embassy said Casandra didn't need to come so I was alone on this trip. Casandra stayed back with a sitter. It was my first visit there and it was a long, 12-hour train ride! As soon as I could get off the train. I made my way to the subway, then to my exit and a couple of blocks to the embassy safe. As I walked in there, I told myself *Daddy owns this, and everyone in it.*

When I entered, I checked in at the first window with my correct paperwork and itinerary for Casandra's plane ticket. *Certainly they won't deny her visa if I already bought her ticket, right?* The kind lady behind the window reassured me that I could *not* turn the itinerary in with the paperwork. *Yikes!*

After I sat in a chair, I nervously waited for them to call me. The embassy had a smell of a library and everything was made of wood. It looked historic. I remember watching the Romanians going up to different windows one at a time. There were ones who got approved to enter the States and ones who didn't. I prayed like crazy for each person working there on the other side of the glass windows; praying they would have favor on us and approve Casandra's visa, as earnestly as I could.

As I stared at the people and analyzed the embassy employees, another little window suddenly opened. Behind it was a young lady who I hadn't prayed for yet. All of a sudden, my name was called. I gulped. It was my turn.

The young lady greeted me. She was younger than I thought someone working there would be. Her bright, smiling face was reassuring. She had my folder of documents and looked like she had already gone over them. She asked me a few questions about my relationship with Casandra. I answered them to the best of my knowledge. Then, as quick as that she closed the folder and told me she was approving Casandra's visa to visit America. She returned the documents to me and I basically freaked out. A man was passing by behind her and he gave me a *huge* smile. It was like he knew something. I thanked her over and over, and she told me to come back at noon to pick Casandra's visa up. That was that!

Electricity filled my body! Casandra was going to America! God is so good! After exiting the embassy, I called a few Romanian friends to tell them the great news during my wait and we celebrated over the phone together.

When it was time for me to pick up her visa, I stood in line with those who got approved. When it was my turn. I stated Casandra's name and the officer couldn't find her passport. She looked again and didn't see it. She told me to come back in three more hours and that it must not be done processing.

Honestly, my mind started to worry. I got sick to my stomach once again. *Maybe they changed their minds?* I worried that they came to their senses and realized they shouldn't allow this young girl to take a little Romanian child to America for a visit. After all, they didn't know me! Those three hours were horrid. I sat on steps close to the embassy nervously waiting some more. The steps got cold, and then I would pace. Then I would sit, and then I would pace. Despite my stomach ache, I had to trust God.

When it hit the time to be back, I was the first in line this time to pick up her passport. I stated Casandra's name again to the officer. She smiled and handed me her passport. I opened it. There it was. My baby girl's picture with a pretty visa to go to America! I sat back down on those steps and just stared at it. Then I noticed something. *Wait a minute...* I knew my request was only to bring Casandra for a two-month visit. They put an expiration date on this visa. Her visa didn't expire for 10 years. They gave my baby girl a 10-year visa! Even as I am writing this, the 10 years still have not passed yet.

It was a kiss from Heaven. He was reminding me that He could do much more than I even prayed for. God surely was in control. He was being so good to us! The fight was real, but the product was more than we imagined. The Bible tells us in Ephesians 3:20 that God is able to do *exceedingly abundantly* more than we can ask or imagine according to the power that works within us (which is His power). A 10-year visa was exceedingly abundantly more than I never imagined they would give her, that's for sure!

Chapter 21

Surprise Visit

For our trip home, I decided to make it a surprise. The only people I told were Crystal, my brother and his wife. That was it. My brother worked in San Francisco, and I wanted him to be the one to pick us up at the airport since he was already there. His task was to somehow arrange for my mom, dad and sister to be in the same place for when we got there with the surprise. My brother called our second family meeting ever. My sister, mom and dad had no idea why.

We were packed and we were ready to grace the land of America. I gathered the documents and made sure I had our passports. Less than 10 minutes out of Oradea, we were at the border of Hungary to head to the airport in Budapest. It was so early it was still dark outside. We pulled up to get our passports stamped to officially leave Romania.

Once the policeman examined our passports he told me that it wasn't possible for me to take Casandra out of the country.

I handed him all of the documents from the child protection agency, her birth mother's approval, and whatever else I had to reassure him that we had been cleared.

The policeman started to get very angry and claim that I could not take Casandra out of the country over and over. A calmer, younger policeman made way to us for help. Our driver made sure they knew it was all approved and was possible. We waited and waited. I prayed and prayed. The knot in my stomach grew and grew.

The young police officer came to me to ask a few questions. He spoke English and I answered all of his questions. I was sure to tell him that we had every single piece of paper we were supposed to have. He then went into the small border office to talk to the irate officer.

We couldn't hear them very well, but we could see them very clearly. The young officer was calmly letting the other officer know it was okay for us to pass. He didn't like it. I could see the battle. All of a sudden, the livid officer through all of my documents in the air. The other officer calmly gathered them. My eyes widened in shock as I watched. After he had each one in hand, he headed our way and brought our passports stamped! *That was intense.*

When we got to the Hungarian border, they just stamped our passports with no questions asked. We drove straight through. I remember counting all of the borders we had to go through at the airports still thinking this could go south. I had a bit of fear. Like I already mentioned, there were times when we had the green light, but something bad happened, like the Easter visit. I also knew that God had big plans for Casandra. The battle raged in front of us and we had to pray through, step by step.

Faith in Jesus isn't about things going the way they were planned. Faith in Jesus means we trust Him no matter what happens. There are many things that we won't understand or see on this side of Heaven. No matter what happens, we have to believe that He is who He said He is. We have to believe His eyes are set upon those who walk upright. Like the Bible says, His arm is not short. He has the reach to touch everyone and everything to line up with His will.

Three years is a long time to not touch the soil of my home country. I never expected it to be that long of a wait. Inch by inch, I couldn't wait to pass the checkpoints to freedom. The Budapest airport was familiar to me. Because it is a small airport, there was no missing the place where I anxiously waited for a ride that one snowy day. Casandra was at my side this time, and I couldn't get to America fast enough.

Again, our passports had to be stamped when it was time to board our flight to our first stop in Paris. We waited aboard the plane for some time and I started to worry because we didn't have much time for our connecting flight. Our flight departed late, which gave us less time.

When we did arrive in Paris, we had to run through the airport to catch our flight. I held Casandra's three-year-old hand, encouraging her to move quickly. My backpack was bobbing up and down on my back. We passed a police officer with a patrol dog. When Casandra saw the dog, she shouted, "Look a doggy! I want to pet the doggy!"

Casandra had a love for animals, and when I had to tell her "no" she started to pout like any child would. This made it even more difficult to get to our gate. Soon I could see our gate number and we ran up to it. As I looked up to the large window, I saw our plane just starting to back out of the gate. We stood there, staring out of the glass, watching our plane to America leave.

I cried "NO! We need to get on that flight!"

The airline attendant reassured me that it was impossible to bring the plane back. I explained to him that the flight from Budapest was late and that had been the reason why we didn't make it. He looked at the computer to find another flight for us. He looked up and told me that the next flight to San Francisco was not until the next day. Oh Jesus! This was crazy! The attendant gladly gave us some food vouchers and booked a room for us until the next day. I had to call my brother and tell him that we wouldn't be coming in that day but the next.

We were so close! You've probably heard this saying: "the struggle is real." Well, let me tell you the struggle was so real! I hated to think it, but I wondered what else could go wrong? I was tired; I was sweating from running across the airport. I had to wait 24 hours longer than expected. I felt like I was dreaming a bad dream.

Casandra wasn't her normal bubbly self when we reached our hotel, and I could tell she was coming down with something. When we got into our room, I realized my baby girl was coming down with a fever. I kissed my sweet girl's forehead and told her,

"I guess we will not go see the Eiffel Tower tonight. Pairs will have to wait for another day for us to grace her with our presence."

That night, I didn't sleep at all. I was so afraid we wouldn't wake up and we'd miss our flight again the next day. Any mother knows when their young child is sick there is not much sleeping anyway. Every half hour I looked at the clock and felt Casandra's' little forehead to see if her fever was rising. One of the last things I grabbed from our apartment in Romania before we left was a small bottle of children's fever reducer. Thankfully I had something to give her, but her fever never broke that night.

Finally, morning came and we actually made it to our flight on time with no hiccups. Casandra slept most of that flight, but woke up not feeling well a few times. I asked a flight attendant if she had any children's medicine to give her and she did. She also brought extra juice and even had a popsicle for her. Poor girl. She was so out of it. My baby girl was normally wide-awake and on the go. *Oh, how I want to be off this plane with her in America.*

Our plane eventually landed and we headed to get our luggage, then on to customs. I knew that security wouldn't reject us, but negative scenarios still fought for attention in my head. The officer opened Casandra's passport and saw her visa. She looked at her while she was laying her head on my shoulder (since she still didn't feel good), and then let us through.

"Welcome back to America," she said with a smile.

That welcome was more of a relief than she knew! I got a cart for our luggage, sat my sick baby girl on it and headed out. My brother was right where he was supposed to be with open arms to meet his niece for the first time. Casandra already loved her uncle before she met him in person. During the moment they met, you couldn't tell she was sick. When she saw her uncle, she ran right into his arms.

My grandmother lived in between San Francisco and my hometown and we wanted to make her house the first surprise. By this time, she and my aunt had already made it to visit us twice. My sweet grandma prayed for us every day. I had Casandra knock at the door and my grandma opened it. There was a little, three-year-old, curly-haired girl standing at the door. My grandma was so happy! She didn't know what to do with herself. After lots of hugs and kisses, we had her call my aunt who lived in that town too. She asked her to come over right away. Casandra and I hid in the family room. My aunt arrived within minutes because of the urgency in my grandma's voice. My aunt walked through the door and we had Casandra peer out of the family room. As soon as she spotted Casandra, my aunt dropped to her knees and started to cry her eyes out. I showered and changed clothes while my aunt and grandma got some love from our little Romanian.

After the experience at my grandma's house, I decided there was nothing quite like surprise joy. I had to remember that my family was patiently waiting for us for all of these year as well! They, too, had to struggle with the adoption process lasting as long as it was. Soon we were off for more surprise visits. We picked up my sister-in-law (who was pregnant at the time) and nephew to head to my dad's house. Before my nephew could get into my arms, he said, "Auntie you, look so beautiful." My nephew was a baby the last time I had seen him in person.

All of those years away from him, but he knew me. *I can't wait to see him and Casandra together.* The rest of my family was at my dad's, waiting for my brother's mysterious "news."

We had Casandra knock on the door of my dad's house while holding my nephew's hand. The door opened. My mom, dad and sister were standing in the living room. When they saw us, they all started to cry. My mom was basically freaking out, my daddy had tears rolling down his checks in an instant and my sister tackled Casandra with hugs and kisses. Three years later... three years! *I can't believe we pulled this surprise off!* It was epic.

The first couple of days were spent recouping from the travel. Jet lag was always worse coming back to the States. Casandra had a fever for a couple of days still, but eventually started to feel better. Once she was better, it was off to explore more in America.

At my dad's house, in the backyard, there is a giant pecan tree. He had a swing hanging from it. Casandra and I were in the backyard just enjoying life. That swing became her favorite. She was fearless and wanted to always, "Go higher, Momma." I would take off running and push the swing as fast as I could. The rush of the upswing would make her giggle with joy. For a moment I stopped to stare at her swinging back and forth. The breeze whisked across her smile and blew her hair around. As I saw those brown, curly locks flying in the wind, I was reminded of the dream I'd had about her. Here we were, three years later after my Mother's Day dream at my dad's house. She was the same age in my dream and those curls were unmistakable. They were the same ones in my dream. It was also summer time, just like in my dream!

Our Lord is so wonderful! More than ever I realized that our great God is the one who sees us and can literally see our future. How amazing is He that He would give me a ten-second glimpse of our future in a dream!?

By this time, Crystal married her boyfriend Josh and had a baby girl named Amaya. It was a blessing to spend time with them. They took us to Disneyland, the beach a half dozen times and even to the San Diego Zoo. Amaya and Casandra started their bond on this trip. What a treat they gave us!

Casandra and I were there to celebrate Amaya's first birthday. We couldn't ask for more. We loved God's timing of it all. Casandra and Amaya were only two years apart and loved each other so much.

We enjoyed much-needed family and friend time. No matter how great things were being back, I still had a knot in my stomach that I had to fight every day. The knot would tell me, *it's not over*. The knot would remind me, *she doesn't carry your last name*. It was a knot that came against my strength and faith. I still had to fight the anxiety. Anxiety would show up when I didn't have an answer to the common question, "When will the adoption be over?" It was anxiety that would creep up to my throat, making me lose sleep. I had to relentlessly remind myself that God said what He said and will do what He needs to do. I had to fight the question, "WHY IS IT TAKING SO LONG?" This question was something I constantly asked Jesus about. And immediately after asking, I would constantly have to lift my hands in surrender, knowing He was going to do it is His time.

Casandra really liked it in America, but I could tell she missed being back in Romania. After two months of our visit, I was ready to go and finalize this adoption. The visit had given me some rest, but I was eager to get back to complete whatever else we had to do.

With this focus, we were back on a plane to Romania. The trip back was much different. Casandra was full of spunk and character, obviously feeling much better on this plane ride. I was tired and closed my eyes for a minute after we had taken off. I woke up a few minutes later and saw that she was not in her seat. She was climbing the back of her chair! I quickly pulled her little legs down and reminded her to stay in her seat. She just giggled at me. I couldn't help but notice the other people on the plane giggling from her sweet smile. It was hard to be upset with her because she was so funny and full of life. This 12-hour plane ride back to Paris was going to be a long one!

Chapter 22

Questions Unfold

Changes were happening in Romania as a whole. The European Union was growing, and Romania desperately wanted to be a part of it. The main reason was for the finances they would gain. There were a few adjustments Romania was required to do in order to enter the EU after they assessed the country. The main adjustment the EU wanted fixed was Romania's "orphan problem." The European Union made it clear to them that something had to be fixed.

Thousands of children in the hospitals and orphanages around this country could not go unnoticed. Because most of these children were not officially abandoned, they were not officially "orphans." Their birth parents still had parental rights just as Casandra's birth mother had before she signed the paper for her parental rights to be terminated. Many left their children in these places (supposedly) to pick them up again when they were of working age. It became a culture of neglect. Many wondered why it had come to this. Most say poverty, but truth be told, no one knows.

The grand idea Romania had was to close the orphanages. They closed them by taking each child, one by one, and dropping them off at their last given address on file. This was put into place in hopes that their parents would take care of them. This is what "reunification" looks like with no wisdom or compassion attached to it. I'm sure anyone reading this is as opposed as I was about this absurd, grand idea.

That was the best plan that the leaders of Romania could think of to fix their problem? To shut down orphanages? Because Romania was under the European Union's pressure, I believe their plan was not well thought out. First off, that was a lot of babies to bring back. Second, most of their parents were probably not at their last given address. I learned that one the hard way through the search for Casandra's birth mom. Third, and most importantly, what if the parents didn't even want them back at their homes? This wasn't rocket science. This was common sense.

I must also mention that 90% of orphans in Romania were of Roma (Gypsy) descent. They are very nomadic. Romanians know this. It's not a secret. The chance of the parents actually being in the village the child was from was slim.

The news of the plan spread. Workers and volunteers in the child protection arena started to hear about it. One day, it became a nightmare. Sure enough, the babies started to leave. A couple children at a time were taken by an ambulance to the address they had on file. I don't know what happened to most of the babies, but I do know of a horrendous story that happened to one.

Maria was about 20 months old. She had spent most of her days in a crib in the hospital. You could make Maria smile in a second, which was not the case for most children growing up in these conditions. She was vibrant and had a little spunk. Volunteers were there to love her and play with her. One young lady who I knew was fond of her. She knew it was only a matter of time before they would take Maria from the hospital and drop her off at the last address they had on record. The day came for Maria, and Maria was gone.

Not even a week had passed, and the young lady who loved Maria very much had called me hysterically crying. Through her sobs and weeping, she told me that someone had found Maria in a ditch covered with cigarette burns, barely alive. I could hear the great pain in her voice and it took less than a second for my eyes to flood with tears. It felt like a nightmare. How could this happen?

I went to see Maria as soon as I could and to be there for my friend. Maria was in her crib when I got to the children's hospital. Maria's smile had dimmed. It wasn't there. She looked at me with a gaze I didn't recognize through the rails of the white crib. My heart broke and the tears fell. It was the saddest, most horrific thing I had ever seen done to someone or ever experienced before. I wanted to reach out and comfort Maria, but was afraid to touch her. I was afraid if I touched a burned spot, it would put her little body in agony. She was covered in deep burns on her face down to her toes.

How could someone do this? I was red-hot angry and I was heartbroken. Poor little Maria was hurting; she was in so much pain. Not just in her body, but also through her eyes I could see the pain of her soul. I was mad at the person, the fully evil person who did this, but I was equally disheartened at the decisions this country made that put Maria in such danger. She could have easily lost her life. Thank God someone had found her!

One story is enough to realize this was a crazy idea. It's not a plan that considered the health and safety of these little lives at all. It's not a plan that thought about Maria's future. It was awful I tell you, awful. Maria's story is not forgotten through the pages of this book. I'm not sure where she is now, but I pray her internal and external scars have lightened. I don't want any scars to remain to remind her of that horrendous day.

That night I held Casandra a little tighter. This was one of the nights when I cried myself to sleep. I couldn't help but wonder where Casandra would have been if she, too, had been one of the children dropped off at her last address. I just held her.

"Mommy, why are you crying?" she said.

"Mommy just loves you so much baby. I just love you so much," I told her as I looked into her eyes. She smiled and brushed off my tears.

"It's okay, Mommy. I love you too."

Eventually, I found out the foundation that first started to help me was doing the same. They were taking the children in their care and dropping them off at their last given addresses. Had Casandra been under their foundation, they would have come and got her at four years old. They would have taken her to the last address they had on file. Since I know for a fact there was no one there to take her at that last given address, would my baby have ended up like Maria?

The times when I didn't understand and felt so alone, those were the times when God was actually watching over us. It took years for me to understand it, but He was in reality hiding Casandra in the shadow of His wings by making those plans *not* work out. My first instinct was to fight to get something accomplished, but this sums it all up: God was looking out for us. Instead of ashes, He was giving us beauty and life.

Days turned to weeks and weeks turned into months.

Eventually, I met up with Sandra from England again. Through the grapevine, I heard she might have new information for us. She continually pushed through her walls of adoption, too. Sandra shared with me that she had sent a "memoir" of her story with her child she was trying to adopt to the main Child Protection office at the capital. She encouraged me to do the same. It was a thorough letter, sharing the entire story of being with that child – when they first met until that day and everything in between.

I worked on one too, writing out every aspect of our four years of time together. I wrote about how Casandra and I had met. Included was our trip to America and all of the times in between. I made sure how much I loved her was clearly known. When every detail was written, my dear friend, Monica, translated it into Romanian for me. She was happy to do it! Monica was very bright and translated it within a few days. After it was ready, I got it notarized and sent it off to the headquarters of Child Protective Services in Bucharest, Romania. Then more of the waiting game came.

Months later after the memoir was in the mail, my laptop was on the fritz. I had a friend come take a look at it who was into computers. He gladly came over to work on the computer. Because I had no idea what he was doing and obviously couldn't help, I decided to go check my mailbox while Casandra was napping. I hardly ever had mail. I don't even know why I was so anxious to look in my mailbox that day. As I opened my mailbox, there sat a single letter. I started to open it as I headed back to the elevator up to my apartment. It was a letter in formal Romanian. Even though my Romanian was getting much better, unfortunately I could not understand most of it. I walked through my apartment door and handed it to my friend to read. He read it and said:

"Oh! You got it!"

"Got what?" I asked.

"The thing you wanted – you got it! You got the permission to stay in the country!"

Oh, what gladness this letter brought me. The letter basically said that they received the "memoir" and were granting me the card I needed to adopt Casandra. It was signed and officially stamped by the Director of Child Services of Romania as well as the Chief of Police in Bucharest. I stared at those beautiful signatures, picturing actual people signing them. They were so beautiful. They were so real.

My normal day turned into another pivotal day marked by the hand of God. I didn't know the faces behind these signatures. I didn't know who decided it was best to allow me to get my permission to stay. I will never know. What I do know is that another miracle had occurred in Casandra's life and she was too young to even understand all of it.

The very next day, I headed to the police station to start the process to get the permanent residence card. The two men who worked in this office in Oradea were the ones working that day, like usual. They both knew my face well – the same guy who processed Casandra's passport and the same guy who kept turning me down. I had been in there plenty of times trying to figure this whole thing out. They saw me coming.

I told them I was there to get my permit to stay card. The shorter of the two said, "I told you! You need to be here for five years!" Eagerly I said, "I know, but they gave it to me. Here is the letter!"

After handing him that letter with a smile beaming from my face, he read it, and under his breath he told his partner, "They are giving it to her." He explained that he didn't know how, but the letter was officially stamped and notarized giving me permission to get the card!

The process to get my permanent resident card had started. I filled out the form, paid my dues, took my picture and waited for it to come. They told me the card would take a few months to process. I made sure I hung on tight to the paper signed by the chief of police just in case.

Thank God for Sandra! Thank God she fought for her son and helped with this piece of our story. Thank God for favor with the chief of police and in the child protective service in Bucharest. Thank God for Ciprian as well. He was very happy for me when I was able to show him proof of the resident card. Because this piece of the story's puzzle was over, we were sure on the home stretch.

Chapter 23

Myspace Love

My baby girl was getting older. By this time, we had spent four of her birthdays together, going on five. Every year away from us, Crystal managed to send a birthday-themed box for me to decorate for Casandra's birthdays. One of her favorites was "The Little Mermaid." Crystal sent 100 turquoise balloons for me to blow up and cover our living room for an under the sea birthday party. When Casandra and I were out and about, she would stop and sing to a lady she was fond of who sold flowers near the apartment. She loved to sing "Part of Your World" to her. The lady would clap while telling her she had no idea what she was singing since it was in English, and then hand her a beautiful, red rose. Casandra would bow, as we would clap for her.

She was the light of my life! Casandra was super busy, always funny and on the go. There were many moments that I would wonder what it would be like to share our life together with someone. She was certainly taken care of, but a daddy would do her a whole lot of good.

Sometimes, when I would be making dinner, I would imagine what it would be like if God put my future husband in our lives. Images of him playing with Casandra while I cooked for us appeared. As I longed for her adoption to be over, I also longed for a daddy for her; a daddy who loved her like I do. We even made up a little song that went like this:

"Boom boom, ain't it great to me Momma.

Boom boom, ain't it great to be Casandra.

Boom boom, ain't it great to be a family.

Boom Boom, and we're praying for a daddy."

After singing it, we would giggle and I would give her smiling face a huge hug!

One day, I took Casandra out of the apartment to get fresh air and to kick a ball around in the little grass area that was near our neighborhood. A woman had asked me what I was doing in Romania and I made conversation with her. She told me that I shouldn't be wasting my youth by taking care of an orphan. Little did she know that my destiny was to do that very thing in my youth: to love Casandra. She asked if I was married. When I told her no, she asked me, "What if your future husband does not love her?" I simply shared that he would not be the one for me if he did not love her. I knew the woman didn't mean any harm. After all, this was my life, in Romania. Many people didn't understand me and I was confronted by it often.

My theory on the daddy issue was that not everyone was cut out to fit our already made family. I was not worried by the worries of others in the situation. I trusted God. He would bring my husband to us at the right time. I knew he would love her. The fact that I knew he would, still didn't change the strong desire to find him...sooner rather than later. I would think about him and pray for him, even though I didn't know his name.

God asked me one time what I wanted in a husband. I prayed for a man who loved God more than anything. I also prayed that he would be tall and from California. No joke! Those were the first three things out of my mouth in my husband conversation with God. I also told Him I wanted someone who would fight for me. From this day forward, a guy who didn't fight for me was out. *If a guy doesn't fight for me, he's not the one for me.* He had to be a man whose actions matched his words.

During the summers, youth organizations would bring teens on mission trips just like my first time to Romania. There were two young girls who had recently moved to Romania for a year after coming on a short-term trip first. Sarah and Devin were sweet and full of passion for the Lord. I would spend time with them and help them when I could with living life in Romania. It was the era when the social media trend was to use Myspace. The girls both had accounts and couldn't believe I didn't have one. I had no desire for one.

They talked about the benefits and encouraged me to get one for weeks. They were relentless! Eventually, I gave in and got one. I was under the impression Myspace would be a better way to help me keep in contact with friends and family. Sarah and

Devin still joke about how it took me an hour just to choose my profile picture! I picked a cute one of me holding Casandra as she smelled a beautiful flower.

They were right...it was nice finally being plugged into the online social world. I could see what my friends and family were up to back home and could write them brief messages. I set a strict rule for myself: never accept a friend request from someone I didn't know, just to be safe. Every time a friend request came from a stranger, I would quickly deny him or her. It sounds harsh, but that was my rule.

In May of 2006, I was checking my friend requests area and there was one. An "AIR-RICK" to be exact, who had a picture of a pier at a beach. *I mean really?!* I obviously didn't know this person. *Who would put a picture of a beach on his profile pic anyway?!* I quickly went to press the "deny" button and my elbow slipped, accidently pressing the button to be this "AIR-RICK's" friend. I swiftly went into my friends list to unfriend him because like I said, I had a rule!

Then, I had a thought. *Hmmm, maybe I do know him. Hmmmmmm, let me check out his page to know for sure if I do or don't.*

With a click on his profile picture, I was on his page. Starting with his blurb all about him. I was surprised when he wrote about God and his faith a lot. Then I checked his pictures out to see if he had another nature scene or a real picture of him. After looking, he did have pictures of himself. He was cute too, but I didn't know who he was. I was curious why he asked to be my friend and how he found my profile. At that moment,

I did something I would consider brave. I mean, traveling the world when you're 20 by yourself, sure, I had that. But writing this so-called Air-rick person, I was a little leery.

I did it. I wrote, and I quote:

"Um......Hi"

He wrote back, and then I wrote back. I asked him how he "found" me on Myspace. To my excitement, he was going on a mission trip to (guess where...) Romania a month later and wanted to ask people who lived there about the country. I was one of those people. After a few messages, Air-rick gave me his real name: Erik. We continued to write back and forth day and night. Romania is ten hours ahead of California time. My night was his day and his day was my night. I couldn't wait to wake up to find another message from him. That went on for a month. We talked mostly about God, Casandra and Romania. Then our messages turned into phone conversations.

Crystal decided to spend the summer in Romania that year, and she got to experience it all. Crystal brought Amaya, who was two years old now with her. This was one of the best summers of my life. Casandra and Amaya played in the summer sun, we ministered to people and I was about to meet a guy who I total had a crush on.

After Crystal saw me getting ready in the morning only to talk to Erik on Skype, she said, "You are in a frenzy!" I would hustle to get ready and then sit at the computer before our day began. First, there would always be an email or a message from him on Myspace. I would read it and wait to talk to him. He would tell me about his day and I would tell him what we had planned for ours. Erik was on a dodgeball team with friends from his church and he would tell me all about the amazing plays of the game. He would leave right after the game to get on Skype to talk to me. His friends started giving him a bad time about not hanging out after the games. When he told me that, I started to get the sense that he was starting to like me as well.

Crystal and I would talk about if he was the one for me. I was not sure. I mean, yes, I was starting to really like him just by talking to him and messaging with him. I was just left in wonder.

His arrival to Romania was getting close. He was going to be located in a town I had never heard of. It was six hours away. Since he couldn't come to the town I was living in, he asked me to come visit him. I did the only thing a girl who liked this guy would do! I rented a car, got a map (yes, a paper map) and headed to him.

As you can already tell, Erik loved God very much. He was from California, but here is the crazy part: Erik is 6 feet 5 inches tall! Now, that is tall! It was nice to know other people from his church were coming, too. Some were his really good friends. I was glad that it wasn't a random trip to Romania by himself. That would be scary for me to be alone, meeting a random man alone like that. Since he was with a team from his church, I felt like it was safe. I was also glad that Crystal would be with me. Plus Casandra and Amaya kept each other company.

Before Erik ventured to Romania, we figured out when I would be able to go visit: during the last part of his two-week trip. I told him that when he was in Romania, I didn't want to keep contacting him every day – not until we were on our way to go see him. I wanted God to be able to speak to him or touch his heart about a possible life in Romania. After all, I had been there for five years! I didn't know when Casandra's adoption was going to be finalized. Only God knew.

The day of his arrival came, and after his flight across the world, he was finally in Romania. I was so excited that the guy I was falling for was now only a few hours from me. The days ticked by, getting closer to when we would see each other face to face. One evening, I got a random call from a phone number I didn't recognize. It was Erik! "Hey, you're not supposed to call me yet!" I guess he was too excited (like me), knowing the day we were supposed to meet was coming up. We had gone from talking everyday to not hearing each other's voices for seven days. That was long enough. He talked about how much he loved their trip so far and what the team had been doing. It was nice to hear his voice and the excitement in it.

Crystal and I found out there was a medieval festival in Sighisoara, which was a town about an hour from where Erik was. We decided to head to the festival a day before Erik and I were meeting up. We loaded up the car and were on our way. Our girls had a blast at the festival! They ate ice cream, got their faces painted and Casandra picked out a unique gift for Erik: she chose a wooden sword and shield. She wanted her own so they could play together.

After the festival, we headed to the town Erik was in to stay the night. Crystal and I rented a room at a small villa. We couldn't meet up with him until the next day, since his team was ministering at a youth camp that evening. Honestly, it gave me a little more time to prepare my heart.

After finding some dinner and settling in, it was time for bed. Crystal and the girls had fallen asleep easily after the car ride and fun-filled day. I, however, could not sleep. *Could I actually be meeting my future husband tomorrow?* There was such a peace in my heart even though it did have a few butterflies in it...peaceful butterflies. I tossed and turned and decided that I would write Erik a letter. Restless, I got up and grabbed a pen and paper.

Maybe writing would put my heart to rest so I could finally go to sleep. In my heart, I sensed Erik was the one who God had picked out for me, but I didn't want to get my hopes up or move things along too quickly. This would be a letter I planned to keep for a while, giving it to him on a special day. Someday, I wanted him to know that before I even laid my eyes on him in person, I believed God had sent him to me.

This is what I wrote:

Erik, July 27th, 2007

Hi, Love! It's the day before I get to meet you in person, and I decided to write to you tonight and give it to you on a special day in the future. I can't get you out of my mind and heart. I know without a doubt that God is up to something. When I think of you, I think of how perfect you are for me and how you're everything I desire in a person who I will spend the rest of my life with. Tomorrow is the first day we meet, but it's also the day that for the rest of my life, no more wondering, no more not knowing who God has for me. I'm basically writing this because I know I saw you before tomorrow. I'm sure by now I have explained every little detail to you so this should make sense to you. I don't know where we are in our relationship right now as you read this, but I want to tell you to keep loving God more than you love me, because if I still love God more than anyone too, we must be doing pretty good.

I can't wait until you hold me. I can't wait until we get to cuddle Casandra together before she goes to bed. I can't wait to hug you and close my eyes and listen to your heart. I can't wait to see the world with you. Before you came to Romania, I called you and read Psalm 46. In verse 10 it says, "Be still and know that I am God. I will be exalted among the nations." Let's allow God to use us so He will be exalted everywhere we go. Together.

Halie

I put the pen down, folded that little letter away in my Bible and was finally able to fall asleep.

Chapter 24

He Fought for Us

Morning came. We woke up to Casandra chatting away. She told us, "Today is an exciting day, and I get to meet my daddy!" Crystal and I were still wiping the sleep out of our eyes. We laughed at that comment! We were surprised she said that! She must have been listening in on one of our conversations, but she didn't skip a beat just like usual.

We got ready for the day and then called Erik. He gave us a time that he would be able to meet and the address to the church he was staying at. We got into the car a little early to get there. We went about three blocks and then made a turn. There it was! We were already there. I was super peaceful until I realized we had only been a few blocks from seeing him that whole time.

I called him on the phone to tell him we were already there and to come outside. Oh my! I was nervous! I'm sure he was nervous as well, since we each thought we had more time until the actual moment we were face to face. I didn't even know what to do. I got out of the car and stood by it, with a million more but-terflies descending on the scene. I didn't know whether I should wait in the car, stand by the car or even where I should place my hands. Pure and simple, I was a mess.

Out of this building he came. He came right up to me, wrapped his arms around me and gave me the biggest hug. The butterflies fluttered away. *He is so tall that his chin rests on the top of my head and I can place my head on his chest to hear his heart. I love that...*

Casandra jumped out of the car to give him a hug too! She was very excited to meet him as well. Erik was with his friend Brian. Brian was the one who encouraged Erik to go on that mission trip to Romania. We said hello to Brian and introduced them to Casandra, Crystal and her little girl Amaya. Later, I found out that Brian raced Erik down the stairs of the church and said, "I'm going to meet your future wife before you!"

Soon after our initial interaction, we got to walk to a nearby park. Casandra immediately longed for his attention. She climbed high on certain structures and waited for Erik to go after her. I just sat back for a few minutes and watched these two inter-act very intently. Erik tried his best to engage in Casandra's game. These two were hitting it off pretty well.

A while later, we went to the church where Erik's team was staying. We got to meet his friends on the team, and Casandra started to get more energetic. The local pastor's wife was bring-ing the team's dinner out for the evening. She placed a platter of chicken legs on the table. Casandra eyed the chicken, quickly picked up a chicken leg and shoved it in her mouth. I was so embarrassed. "Casi that chicken is for the team! You need to ask before you just take something." I apologized to Erik for her behavior, and he was so sweet and calm. He said it was just from the long day in the car and she was glad to be out! He reassured me, and he was not bothered by what she had just done.

The pastor from the church came in and we were introduced. We spoke a little Romanian together and he told Crystal and I we could stay there if we wanted to. They had another room in the church basement where they could put mattresses in for us. It was a blessing for us, since we were paying a lot for our room at the villa.

The next day, Erik and I got some free time together with his friend Chris. Chris wanted to buy some sunglasses, so the three-of-us went shopping with him. Casandra stayed with Crystal while we went. As we went through a few little shops, Chris tried on a few glasses and Erik and I agreed upon ones that looked best on him. In one shop, I was standing in front of Erik and he whisked his hand across the top of my back. The unexpected touch surprised me and sent a flush across my face. After the glasses were picked out, we went out for lunch together. Crystal, her little girl and Casandra joined us at the cafe. During that lunch, Erik and I talked and talked and talked. We got to know each other in front of each other for a change instead of in front of a computer. We also took a walk and got ice cream. He carried Casandra on his shoulders, and she absolutely loved it!

Later on that night, it was time for bed. The little room in the church that the pastor offered us was perfect. Casandra and I laid on the mattress on the floor reading her favorite book before she fell asleep. Erik sat in a nearby chair as I read to her. As my feet dangled off the side of the mattress, Erik moved his foot to touch mine. Casandra fell asleep.

At this moment in our relationship, Erik had no idea my love language was touch. Those two little gestures to me were not so little. It wasn't strange though; it was comfortable.

Sadly, Erik's plane was leaving for California the next morning with the mission team. Since it was our last evening together until God knew when, we went out on a little balcony and talked until about 3 a.m. when it started to rain…just like in the movies. I hugged him goodbye for the first time and wondered if he was the one who was going to fight for me.

The next day, the girls and I drove back to Oradea. My lack of sleep was certainly worth it, although I could really feel it on our drive. We made it back to home sweet home, and I impatiently waited for Erik to fly across the world and get back to his computer. When he finally got to his apartment in California, we Skyped. I couldn't wait to talk to him! It was in that conversation that he asked to "court" me. I was happy that he took the first step. Our new courtship meant we were committed to each other. I still wasn't positive if he was the one who would fight for me, but I loved the thought of getting to know him more in a romantic relationship…I mean, as romantic as you can get half a world apart.

In our conversation before we met in person, Erik told me he wanted to be a missionary. I had some simple advice for him if he was serious about being a missionary: don't do anything silly, like buy a brand-new truck. "If you're going out on the mission field, you can't be buying expensive things in America that can hold you back." I was certain that *my man* would not do such silly things if his heart was to go to the nations.

One morning, I rushed to the computer to talk to him like I always did. I checked his Myspace page first. To my joy there was a picture of the truck he owned. Right above the picture he wrote, "Truck for Sale!"

Okay everyone…Erik had me at, "I'm going on a mission trip to Romania." He had me at his kind excuses for Casandra's behavior. He had me at the back touch and toe touch. Now he really had me at "Truck for Sale!" Not only did Erik sell his truck, he started selling EVERYTHING he owned; even down to the DVD's and his kitchen table. This guy who loved Jesus, who was from California, who was 6 feet 5 inches was moving to Romania to be with his girls!

I don't know of anyone who would do this or who has ever done this. Many people talk about the things God may have for them; some people may talk about being missionaries and traveling the world for Jesus. Erik was actually doing it. He was doing everything in his power to get to us. He took the biggest leap of faith I have ever seen anyone take, and he was doing it for me. He saw what God put in front of him and dove in head first. He also didn't let anything hold him back.

Little by little he sold his vehicle, furniture and many other things he owned, and I watched and waited. Outwardly he was doing it, but I was cautious, smart enough to know that he could change his mind. When he was in my arms again at the airport, then I would completely believe he was moving to Romania.

Because so many things turned upside down during the adoption process, it was hard to believe it until I saw it.

We continued our relationship over Skype, and during one conversation we had, Erik told me he was buying his plane ticket. The winter had already come and he had decided to come back right smack in the middle of it – in January. This was really happening!

It was August, and he needed time to finish selling everything and get the funds built up to support living in another country. Those five months between August and January without him were tough. We were committed to each other when we chose to court each other, but I saw the commitment he was making for me, to get to me even if there were so many unknowns. It didn't matter to him. He didn't analyze every little detail about the future; he just stepped into it.

After selling his things and paying off debt, he was on a plane to Romania in January just like he said. I went to the airport to pick him up and had someone stay with Casandra. Once I saw his handsome face coming towards me with his luggage, I knew my man had fought with all he had, giving up all he had to be there. Casandra and I were more important to him than the comfortable life Fresno, California, was offering him. This proved to me that we were the most important. I wanted to spend the rest of my life with someone who would do that for us. I was officially in love and finally in his arms.

Gelu and Anca let Erik move in with them while he was there. They are such a giving family. Gelu and Anca are as sweet as they come. We spent a lot of time with each other, and they are the type of people who would offer the shirt of their backs if you needed it. In our case, they offered their couch and Erik accepted.

For six months Erik slept on a couch at their house, and then came over in the morning to be with us. Erik became friends with my Romanian friends and they really enjoyed his company. He also got the chance to see what it was like to be a missionary. For once I had help caring my groceries from the grocery store. It was nice having this tall guy around! Not only that, but Casandra had two more attentive ears to listen to her jokes and silliness. She loved having him with us.

We had our first official date, just the two of us, on Valentine's Day. Sarah was living in Romania at the time and watched Casandra for us. I had never gone out on Valentine's Day before while living here, since I never had a date! We decided to go to my favorite restaurant. To our surprise, the place was packed and there wasn't a spot for us. Who knew Valentine's Day was so popular in Romania! We ended up walking all around town trying to find a restaurant, but everywhere we turned the places were full. The only place we knew of that wouldn't be packed was McDonalds. Tired and hungry, we made our way there. The funny thing was McDonalds was right next to my apartment! We went around town looking for a great place for a date and ended up right back where we started. Despite a little wasted time, I still couldn't believe he was right in front of me. We enjoyed each second with each other even if our plans didn't turn out like we thought for our first date!

Erik got involved in several meaningful projects in our area, such as building a fence for a ministry that cared for children, helping Gelu and Anca feed homeless people living under tunnels and ministering to young adults. He got a good taste of Romania while we were building our relationship and waiting for the adoption to be finished.

I had to help a friend one day and decided to leave Casandra with Erik. I was gone for the morning, and when Casandra heard the door open and close when I returned, she came running down the hall to greet me. Erik, on the other hand, just sat in a chair in the living room on his computer. *I'm back! Aren't you going to greet me too?* I remember feeling a little aggravated with him for not greeting me. So, I went into the kitchen to grab a bite to eat, and then heard a knock at the door.

When I opened the door, my friend Sebastian was there with a pretty bouquet of flowers. He said something about being there to deliver them for me. *What?* I was kind of confused, took the flowers, turned to go down the hall and there was Erik… walking up to me with a ring box! Right there in my hallway he proposed to me. We kissed and of course I said yes. Then, Casandra ran down the hall shouting, "Yes! Mommy and Erik are getting married!" We picked up our precious Casandra and had a group hug full of joy. Sebastian also gave us a celebration hug and headed out.

Erik and I desperately wanted to start our family. We trusted that God was going to pull through on the adoption soon. Ciprian was still working on gathering every last paper for Casandra's adoption. The nervous knot was still in my stomach since it wasn't over yet. It was a waiting game; a long waiting game. In the meantime, I now had my fiancé to lean on and join his faith with mine.

Erik had a return plane ticket booked for six months after his arrival, and the time was quickly approaching. We did not want to separate from each other, but he did have to get back to the States to get a job and start saving money for our future. Erik decided to stay two more weeks than what his ticket allowed. His grandma offered to pay for the fee to change the ticket's departure date, which was a huge blessing! He wasn't going to change the ticket, but when his grandma offered to pay for it, he was relieved.

A day after his ticket was switched, we got a call from Ciprian. Ciprian had the greatest news of all! "Halie, I have an adoption court date for you!" The date was just two days before Erik's new departure date back to the States. The two-week postponement of his flight meant Erik got to be there for the finalization of Casandra's adoption. If he hadn't switched his plane ticket, he would have missed it completely. How great is God, that He did this for us!

Even though this news was fantastic, the knot in my stomach felt like a rock every morning until our court date. *God, You've got this...*

The morning of our court date arrived. We woke up that sunny morning in June ready to get this adoption completed. A few of my friends joined us at the courthouse. I walked in the room with Ciprian and Erik and sat at the large table before us. The judge looked at me and proceeded. "Are you, in fact, willing to adopt Casandra?" I gladly said, "Da!" (which is 'yes' in Romanian). Then, she ordered the adoption to be finalized. That was it. It was over!

I gave Ciprian a huge hug, and Erik and I walked out of that courthouse hand in hand like we were floating on a cloud. My friends were so excited! We were thrilled beyond words! I didn't even know what to do with myself. Erik, Casandra and I rejoiced, but it honestly didn't seem real. *Is that it? After all the heartache, hurdles and years of process, is it really done with a one-minute conversation?*

We walked to an ice cream shop nearby to celebrate. I got my ice cream and sat next to Erik. I had this gigantic feeling of exhale; a rush of deep tiredness flooded my whole body and soul. At that moment, all I could do was lay my head on my love's shoulder. I couldn't keep my eyes open. I told Erik, "I am so tired!"

Exhausted, I barely made it home to my bed. *What is happening to me?* I went straight to my bed and had to sleep; I had to rest! I fell asleep so quickly, which was not normal for me. I'm the type of person who has a hard time taking naps. In fact, I don't do naps. This day, our adoption day, my body was screaming for my bed and sleep. Erik took care of Casandra; I slept.

For five years of my life, my body, mind, will and emotions were in a constant state of fight and struggle. Every single day I fought the *what ifs*. There was a relentless intensity, and I didn't recognize it as an issue during the fight. I had given my all to this baby girl and her adoption. All my time, my energy, my money and my whole being was dedicated to her. Now that it was finalized, my body was deeply fatigued and needed to shift into a complete state of rest. It was strange. I always imagined Casandra's adoption day being a celebration, a party – the biggest one ever seen. Instead, the way the Lord allowed me to celebrate was in complete rest.

The knot, the yucky, ugly knot in my stomach had disappeared. The rambling, anxious thoughts had to flee, no longer having a foothold. The enemy was silenced. The mouths of the naysayers were silenced. Faith had silenced the faithless. God's Word had not returned void. My God, *my* God was an ever-present help in time of need. His voice was like rushing water and His Holy Spirit counseled me. The towering mountain that was before me was removed.

Erik was able to leave in peace. It was only a matter of time until his girls would be following him across the world back to California. It was hard for us to let him go, but it was easier knowing he was going to get back home and start preparing for our arrival. I had a ring on my finger and our hearts were committed to each other. I took him to Budapest where we took a boat up and down the Danube to see this beautiful city before his flight. We didn't know the exact date we would see each other again, but since the adoption was over, we knew it was only a matter of time.

The only thing left to do was to get our little Romanian a visa to come to America with her new name. Her old passport wasn't valid anymore because she held my last name now. *Praise God for her new name!* We waited for her birth certificate to be printed and it took a month or so. Then, we applied for her new

Romanian passport with her new name. That took time. As soon as we got it, we made an appointment at the American embassy in Bucharest again for a visa. This time, Casandra had to go with me.

While this was going on, I started to sell and give away our things. Our apartment was such a nice place to live that I wanted the right people to move into it after us. As I prayed about this, a couple who had just got married came to mind. Cristian was my friend and he had just married a sweet American girl from California who was living in Romania. Her name was Jenni. I called them and asked if they wanted to take over rent and move into my apartment when we moved back to America. "Well, we like our apartment now and don't really want to move." They declined, but I was sure to let them know that I prayed about it and they came to my mind. "If you change your minds, please let me know."

About a month later, Cristian called me. He shared that the landlord of their current apartment was significantly raising their rent, and now they wanted to take over my apartment. I was delighted to have them. In fact, they moved in with us a month before our embassy appointment. They needed to get out of their apartment soon and everything was working out for everyone.

My busy little girl was now six and did very well on our train ride to the capital. When we entered for our appointment, the embassy was bare. I happily gave the lady at the window all of our documents. "Thank you, I will be back with the decision soon." Casandra and I waited and waited. Thankfully, I brought a book in my backpack to keep her busy, but you can only read a book so many times before a six-year-old gets bored. I did my best to keep her from climbing the fancy, wooden walls and pillars as we waited. *Why is it taking so long?!*

Eventually, the lady who took my papers called me back up. I was expecting a quick approval. The lady shared with me that I was missing a document. The council that was deciding on Casandra's visa wanted the document from the court of Casandra's birth mother's parental rights being terminated. It was a 12-hour train ride from where those documents were. I called Ciprian and found out he was on a trip. He was away from the office and couldn't get to them. Then, I remembered I did have that paper, but it was in Oradea in my drawer at home.

Wait, I can call Jenni! She was at work, but she happily agreed to go back to our apartment to find the document I needed. As quick as she could, she faxed the paper to the embassy. They received it. Casandra and I waited again. During the wait, I felt that old, familiar knot forming in my stomach. *Knot, God has brought us this far and He will not let us lose now.* "Halie and Casandra." The lady called us back up to the window, and with relief in her voice, granted Casandra the visa to enter into the United States of America. God is amazing! He even knew I wouldn't have that paper, but knew Jenni would be able to get it for me if they moved in. He cares about the smallest details of our lives!

We picked up her passport and visa and trekked back to Oradea. This time, when we received her visa, I didn't get tired. My face beamed and I couldn't stop smiling. My love was waiting for us in California. Our little family could now move on with God's next adventure for us.

Chapter 25

Blessing Her Birth Mother

Our last week in Romania was terribly sad. My apartment was different. Cristian and Jenni had put their things into place and my things were going away. What had been my home for so long, didn't look like my home anymore. There was a tug-o-war within me. I could not wait to be back into Erik's arms, but at this point it had been six years of building a life in this nation that I loved. I had to say goodbye to my dear ones, possibly never to see them again. Friends trickled in over the week to say goodbye.

There was a sense of loss. We were leaving the ones who loved Casandra and I until the end, no matter what. I found myself crying tears of joy and tears of sorrow in the same hour. My friends who loved us were ecstatic. They knew the long fight was over. Because they, too, had the chance to spend time with Erik, they wanted nothing more than for us to be reunited with him.

Ciprian, over time, had shared that Casandra's birth mom had two more baby girls. She was doing well and was taken care of by her husband. He was not Casandra's father, however. Since Casandra had accumulated nice things from America like clothes, toys, presents and other things from my sister and family, I asked him if I could meet her and give her Casandra's things that we could not take back with us. After all, her little sisters could use the items.

Never before did I want to meet her until now. The birth certificate was made and my name was on it. There was nothing her birth mom could do now, so I didn't have any fear of her going back on her word. Everything was said and done, and it was time to meet her birth mother now that it was all over. My main reason was so I could see the woman who my baby girl was formed in. I wanted to be able to tell Casandra someday if she ever asked about her. By looking her in the eye and being in her presence, I would have some answers if Casandra ever needed them.

Ciprian and I decided on a certain day for the visit. I collected Casandra's extra things and bought a box full of groceries. Our plan was to not let her know who I was, so Ciprian decided to tell her I was from the foundation. I could speak Romanian now, and it was not as obvious that I was American.

I got a babysitter for Casandra and Ciprian and I traveled about two hours to Daniella – the one who gave birth to my little princess. When Daniella saw Ciprian drive up, she was delighted. She was carrying two buckets of water to her house from the nearby river since she did not have running water in her home.

Daniella beckoned us to follow her inside, and we entered following her smile.

As we walked in, I took a mental note of everything. There were dirt floors and no electricity. The little home had two rooms and there were six people living there: Daniella, her husband, the two girls, her husband's mother, and aunt. They were all living there in the two-room home. The windows were in great condition though. Ciprian told me that another foundation was helping them and bought them new windows.

We carried in the boxes filled with surprises for her family and for Casandra's little sisters. The baby named Sara was laying on a bed on her tummy. Sara was as beautiful as Casandra was. She looked to be about six months old. I looked for her other sister named Soledad, but she was not home at that moment. But, as I started to pull something from a box, a little girl about three years old briskly ran into the home with a big, joyful smile. She had spotted the bright pink Princess Ariel backpack.

As she was coming our way, the grandma smacked her on the head with her bare hand and started yelling at her in the Roma language. It wasn't Romanian, so we could not understand what she was saying. The little girl's smile turned into a frown. Daniella didn't do anything.

Oh man, it took everything for me to sit there and not do anything. I wanted to pick her up and take her home with me, too! The smack was so uncalled for and I tried to hold back tears. She had done nothing wrong. She was just excited to see the new, pretty things inside her house. I looked at Soledad and handed her the backpack. She loved it, so I continued to show her the other items I brought. After I was done showing Soledad what I brought her, I asked Daniella if I could hold the baby. She agreed with a smile still on her face.

I'm holding Casandra's sister. I couldn't believe it. As I cradled her in my arms, I tried to make her smile the same way I did when Casandra was at the hospital. I examined her little features and examined Soledad's smile over her new belongings. Soledad didn't look like Casandra very much, but baby Sara had her eyes.

While I was enjoying the presence of the girls, the lady who hit Soledad on the head leaned over to me and asked, "Is the girl you have beautiful?"

I'm assuming she was asking about Casandra. I just looked at her and told her, "I don't know what girl you are talking about." As she looked at me though, I sensed a jealousy about her. She was a mean woman. They didn't know I had Casandra, but the way she asked about her gave me the creeps.

Daniella was so joyful though for someone in her circumstances. I remember thinking *this is where Casandra gets her spunk.* As we talked, I examined Daniella's features closely as well. I took notice of her hands, her nose, her hair and her skin color. *Casandra got her hands and her personality for sure!* I loved how she was respectful and kept calling Ciprian, "Mr. Ciprian."

We didn't stay long, but I eagerly took in every detail I could. After all, that would have been Casandra's home. Ciprian had a camera with him and took a few pictures while we were there. If Casandra ever wondered, I would have something to show her.

Ciprian drove me home and contentment sat firmly in my soul. I unlocked my apartment door and Casandra ran down the hall to meet me. I hugged her and took an extra glance at her beautiful little face. *The angels have been surrounding her.* Again and again I got to see God's hand on her life. It still bothered me that the grandma smacked Soledad on the head, and hard! It also bothered me that Soledad's mom did nothing about it. Casandra was a busy body...she was always on the go! I painfully got the revelation that Casandra may have been abused if she would have stayed with her birth mother. The man her birth mom was married to was not her birth father. She would have most likely been the odd ball out.

I may not get the whole picture of Casandra's life and the destiny God has placed on it, but this revelation was a piece of it. God rescued her from abuse and death a few times over. I was certain of it and even more so after what I had just witnessed. After this experience, oh how I wished that I had thousands of dollars. I would buy a little house where just Danielle, her girls and her husband could live away from that mean lady.

Chapter 26

The Knot is Gone

I put six years of our lives in four suitcases. Even though there was no way to fit in all our things, there were a few special, familiar things I wanted Casandra to have. Her princess sheets were getting old, but those made it in the suitcase. The book I read to her when Erik's foot touched mine was coming with us. All the clothing we could possibly fit got crammed in.

I picked Casandra up from her last day of kindergarten and everyone gave her hugs. She would always manage to find a little lizard in the yard and place it on her shirt. We laughed when she said, "Momma, I want to take the lizard with me to America." I reassured her that he couldn't make the trip.

Gelu and Anca wanted to take us to the airport, but before we headed out of town, we stopped by Lavi's work. Casandra and I hugged her tight. She was such a strong, loving support for us. Next, we had to cross the border and drive to a little motel near the airport in Budapest. Our flight was leaving quite early the next morning. It snowed that night on our way to the motel that November. It reminded me of when I landed by myself the first winter. *We have so many memories here.* It was much easier crossing the Romanian/Hungarian border this time. I had a birth certificate saying that I was her mother. There was no arguing it. I wasn't scared this time. There was also no day indicated when we had to return. It was pure freedom.

At the motel, Anca and I hugged and cried. When sorrow about leaving started to fill my heart, she reminded me how happy she was about us going home to Erik. That reminder always made me smile. We said our final goodbyes, and they drove safely back home before the snow built up.

It was finished. *How come it hurts so bad to leave though?* For six years, all I wanted to do was leave. I loved living in Romania, but my days here were spent with the knot in my stomach that now didn't exist. I kept picturing Erik's face in my mind when the pain would come. His face was my medicine for the sadness in my heart; sadness for leaving a culture, a country and an exact location where God wanted me for this season.

The time I spent in Romania was unforgettable and life-changing. As I look back, I am so thankful it took as long as it did. Erik and I would not have met if it had been shortened. by a year, and the time we spent with the most precious friends anyone could ask for was priceless.

Family, friends and American flags welcomed Casandra and I at the airport in San Francisco. It was like the end of a movie. We ran toward Erik for a huge hug. I was in his arms again, listening to his heartbeat. We were home.

With my whole heart I believe that God knew Casandra was going to be born. He knew He would need someone crazy enough to say yes to Him, to fly across the world for her. Did you know God has already paved the way through Jesus for you to be His kid? Ephesians tells us it was His pleasure to adopt us through Jesus. It was all part of His glorious plan of grace for us to be His kids. He desires you to know your inheritance and to hear His sweet words toward you. Are you listening?

Ending

Flashes of memories are filling my mind. I can't sleep. The memories are good and some of the memories are bad. The memories. The memories won't stop. My story must get out. My story must be told. I see it clearly now than ever.

If it wasn't for a cousin pleading to go to a concert.

If it wasn't for a friend working security.

If it wasn't for a sweet lady with a giving heart.

If it wasn't for that canceled trip to El Salvador.

If it wasn't for MY team going to Oradea.

If it wasn't for the pastor calling the children's hospital.

If it wasn't for that phone call from Dave.

If it wasn't for the eyes to see the spark on a mission trip in South America from Joe.

If it wasn't for the still small voice.

If it wasn't for the girl who had the baby at 14.

If it wasn't for the orphanage director and social worker that
believed in me.

If it wasn't for the letting go.

If it wasn't for the pain.

If it wasn't for the fast.

If it wasn't for the fight.

If it wasn't for some type of glory.

My story wouldn't be whole. My story wouldn't be told. God,
You are listening.

There once was a girl, who wanted to change the world.
She ended up meeting a baby girl who changed hers, and now
has the opportunity to tell their story of love and God's voice.

Every time I look at Casandra, I'm lost in awe and wonder
about how there was a baby I loved with every piece of me. There
was a baby God sent me to love. There was a baby who I wanted.
There was a baby who God's eyes were fixed on. There was a
baby who God used to form a family. There was a baby who God
moved mountains for.

Crystal and Josh went on to adopt in the states. They
have four children now. Amaya, Brighton, Gabriel and Willow.
Brighton came into their family when he was only a week old
from adoption. Years later, Crystal became pregnant with a boy.
After tossing around names for seven months, they settled on
the name Gabriel. Gabriel was born June 23rd, 2015, exactly 12
years minus a day from when we took the Romanian Gabriel to
his family. But since Romania is 10 hours ahead of California

time, it was June 24th in Romania. We took the Romanian Gabriel to his new family on June 24th. Casandra came home the following day June 25th from the orphanage. After Gabriel was born, we realized what God had done! My dream made sense about seeing Gabriel at my dad's house. Both Gabriel's have very similar features too!

Six months after being back in America, Erik and I got married. It was a beautiful, outdoor wedding and Casandra was our flower girl. Lavi, Anca and Gelu made it from Romania! Before I walked down the aisle, I had Lavi give the letter to Erik that I wrote him the day before we met in person. It's one of our treasures. He had tears in his eyes before I even started down the aisle from reading it.

A year later, I gave birth to our son, Korbin. We knew God was going to give us a baby boy. Because we saw the need for so many children in the world without a family, we went on to adopt two more children from California. Angelee and Jeremiah are biological brother and sister. They fit right in between Casi and Korbin. They came home when they were four and three years old. It wasn't long until we found out they had another sister in foster care. That wasn't okay with us, so we adopted her too! Patrice became our oldest, beating Casandra by a year and a half. She came home when she was 13. She and Casandra quickly became more like best friends than sisters.

Through our kids, God has been revealing to us that we should also live as adopted kids; adopted by Him. Because we're His kids, it means we do hear our Daddy's voice, we have Jesus as the best biggest brother ever and we are no longer alone because of the Holy Spirit. That's our identity! If we can get a hold of these truths, just imagine how we would live our lives to extend God's Kingdom.

So, I declare that you hear the voice of the Lord! May you listen closely and follow what He has planned for your life, then just watch the dots miraculously connect! For there are still mountains that need to be moved.

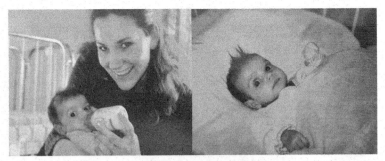

Halie Wood is currently the mission's director of Freedom House Church in Bryon, CA, where she also preaches from time to time. Her messages of faith and being an adopted child of God have touched hearts. She and her husband, Erik, take teams to Romania to minister. They hope to start a non-profit to help orphans find forever families where her heart for children and missions can collide.

Follow the Wood family @WonderwiththeWoods on social media platforms and check out their videos on YouTube.

To contact Halie Wood for speaking engagements or for more information email:

CalledtoCasandra@gmail.com